G000066238

OTHER PEOPLE'S SHOES

KEN JARROLD CBE

OTHER PEOPLE'S SHOES

40 questions for leaders and managers

Published in 2018 by
Other People's Shoes, Stockton-on-Tees

Copyright © Ken Jarrold CBE, 2018

The right of Ken Jarrold to be identified as the author of
this book has been asserted by him in accordance with
the Copyright, Designs and Patents Act, 1988

A copy of this book has been registered with the Library of Congress

All rights reserved. No part of the publication may be reproduced or
transmitted in any form or by any means, electronic or mechanical,
including photocopy, recording, or any information storage and
retrieval system, without permission in writing from the publisher.

ISBN 978-1985879690

Printed by CreateSpace Ltd

Dedication

This book is dedicated to Jack Newton, superintendent of the Royal Hospital in Sheffield. I had the great privilege of being Jack's deputy from November 1971 to May 1974. Jack was a servant manager and leader and showed the way by example.

Acknowledgements

Thanks to everyone I have worked with through the good and the bad times and from whom I have learned so much.

Rennie Fritchie was the second chair I worked with at Gloucester Health Authority and I learned a great deal from her. It has been my privilege to be in touch with her since I left Gloucester at the end of 1989 and I am very grateful to Rennie for reading the draft of this book and offering valuable suggestions.

A very special thanks to Mark Spybey, head of team and people development, and his colleagues at the Northumberland, Tyne and Wear NHS Foundation Trust, rated outstanding by the Care Quality Commission. I have had the extraordinary privilege of sharing these thoughts with them at ten workshops a year since December 2011. The feedback I have received from frontline staff of all professions and occupations has been very valuable in developing my thinking and encouraging me to continue with this work. It has been very gratifying to be told that they have found it useful in their work of caring for people with mental illness and learning disability. I am very grateful to Mark for his help in writing this book.

Many thanks to Zillah Heffer. Zillah and I joined the NHS Administrative Training Scheme on 14 September 1969 as trainees with the East Anglian Regional Hospital Board. In January 2018, after more than forty-eight years of friendship, Zillah contributed challenging and helpful comments on my thoughts and made this a better book.

The purpose of this book is to share with managers and leaders the lessons I have learned from trying to manage and lead. The lessons are summarised in the 40 questions that I hope will help managers and leaders to reflect on their work. Rennie Fritchie suggested that it would be a good idea to answer these questions in dialogue with a colleague that you respect and can trust. This seems to me a really good idea. Reflection with a colleague can be very valuable.

Contents

Chapter One

Definitions of Leadership and Management

What happened

There was a hole in my office carpet when I was Jack Newton's Deputy at the Royal Hospital in Sheffield. I asked Jack if I could have a new one and he said no. I asked why not, and I am sure he heard, in my tone if not in the words I used, that I thought the deputy superintendent of the Royal Hospital, my first job after the NHS National Administrative Training Scheme, should not have a hole in his carpet!

Jack asked me what I would do if a ward sister came into my office (something that happened a lot) and asked me for a new carpet for the ward dayroom and I had to say no because we could not afford it. What, he asked, would the ward sister think when she looked down and saw my new carpet?

If on the other hand, I asked the sister to look down and inspect the hole in my carpet, I would be able to say, "Sister, look at the state of my carpet. Times are hard." The sister would go back to her colleagues and ask if they had seen the state of the poor deputy superintendent's carpet and tell them that she was content to make do with the day room carpet for another year.

What I learned

I learned that the most important people in the hospital were the patients and their relatives and that the next most important people were the frontline staff. The rest of us, including Jack, were there to serve the staff who took care of the patients. We should never have something better than what could be provided for the patients and staff. We were servants first.

What happened

At Cambridge I had the pleasure of knowing Ian Martin. We were both presidents of the Union and later in life Ian was secretary general of Amnesty International and a senior UN official. Ian went from Cambridge to Harvard. In the Harvard bookshop, he came across a first edition of *The Servant As Leader* by Robert K. Greenleaf (RKG). The book was published in 1970 and was the first of Greenleaf's publications following his retirement from AT&T in 1964. It was the beginning of his twenty-six years of teaching and writing, which established him as the founding father of the modern thinking on servant leadership and an influence on many of the best-known thinkers and writers on leadership and management, including Peter Senge, Stephen Covey, Warren Bennis and Kenneth Blanchard. At the very beginning of my work as a manager, when I was forming my aspiration to lead, I had the great benefit of reading RKG's exploration of the *Journey to the East* by Hermann Hesse. Hesse tells the story of Leo, who was the leader, the one who showed the way, but who "was servant first because that is what he was deep down inside... he was servant first".[1]

What I learned

Greenleaf's advocacy of servant leadership instantly appealed to me because it resonated with the values I had acquired from my parents' deep Christian faith (they were missionaries) and which have remained with me in my journey to becoming a Christian agnostic. The concept of service was real to me from my earliest days. However, it was working for Jack Newton that brought RKG's thinking alive for me in the context of NHS management. I now had a theory – a way of thinking – and the

---

1:    Greenleaf, Robert K. *The Servant As Leader* (1970)

practical example of Jack's service to the patients, relatives and front-line staff. I could see what a servant leader and manager could achieve.

Years later I came across a lecture on the leadership principle, given in 1933 by Dietrich Bonhoeffer, the German theologian who lost his life because he dared to stand against Hitler. He said, "The leader must know that he is most deeply committed to his followers, most heavily laden with responsibility towards the orders of life. In fact, quite simply a servant."[2]

Leadership and Management are very different things.

It is very unhelpful that many people, in their writing and speaking, do not define leadership and management, and use the terms interchangeably. If we are to have any chance of learning to lead and manage we need to understand what we are trying to do. RKG said:

- If the word "leader" is a mere synonym for boss it has no meaning at all.[3]
- Many occupy positions of great authority and contribute little to leadership.[4]
- No one should be made a supervisor to whom the workers do not go for guidance and council before they are supervisors.[5]
- A leader is one who goes out ahead and shows the way.[6]

Management is very different. Management is the responsibility for the use of resources. It was easy to see and understand this, and the Thwaites report in 1989 on the education and training of managers in the NHS reinforced my thinking and provided the definition:

> To summarise, we can say that, in any given organization, the title [of manager] should be reserved for those employees

---

2:   Bonhoeffer, Dietrich. *The Nazi Rise to Power: The Leadership Principle. No Rusty Swords. Letters. Lectures and Notes 1928–1936 Collected Works Volume 1* (1965)

3:   Senge, Peter. Introduction to Frick, Don M. *Robert K Greenleaf: A Life of Servant Leadership* (2004)

4:   Senge, Peter, in Frick. Op. cit.

5:   Greenleaf, Robert K. Correspondence to Dr Donald Cowling (1935), quoted in Frick. Op. cit.

6:   Greenleaf, Robert K. Op. cit.

who deploy the resources of the organization. They 'manage' human, financial, physical and informational resources, and they have some impact upon the organisation's good name and the use made of its power and influence. They also manage the structure and operations of the organization itself.[7]

From RKG, and from Jack Newton's example, I began to understand what leadership is. Leadership is showing the way – showing what to do next. I could see that Jack was not only the manager of a 440-bed teaching hospital, accountable for the people, the buildings, the equipment and the finances. Jack was also a leader because through his own behaviour he showed how managers and leaders ought to behave.

I began to see that leadership is not dependent on role and seniority. Leadership can come from anyone who shows the way. This can be seen in the lives and examples of the famous and also in our everyday experience. In many teams leadership does not come only, or even mainly, from the manager. James L. Webb of NASA made this point very well when he said that "the most important person in the room is the one who knows what to do next."[8] The manager controls the resources but may not be able to lead – to show the way. The leader, if they are not also the manager, will need the manager to help make a reality of the direction they are setting, because the manager can make things happen.

John Kotter, believes that leadership is different from management: "The fundamental purpose of management is to keep the current system functioning. The fundamental purpose of leadership is to produce change."[9]

We burden managers with the expectation of leadership. Of course, the best situation is where the leader is also the manager, because the person showing the way has control of the resources needed to follow

---

7: Thwaites, Dr Bryan. King's Fund Working Party on The Education and Training of Senior Managers in the National Health Service. King's Fund (1977)

8: Harrell Leith, J. *The Peace Officer's Companion: 365 days' Worth of Wisdom with Modern Commentary for Today's Peace Officer* (2011)

9: Kotter, John. *What Effective General Managers Really Do*. Harvard Business review (1999)

the way. It is perfectly acceptable for the manager not to know the way provided that they allow other members of the team to show the way and as long as they are willing to be followers. If a manager places their authority and resources in support of leadership of others, this has a very good impact. Not only will the team have a direction, they will see that the manager is willing to follow the way shown by others and will be encouraged to show leadership themselves. It may be that the manager will learn leadership from those members of the team who are allowed to lead.

The worst situation is when a manager cannot themselves lead and prevents others from leading. They may act in this way out of fear of being undermined or shown up. They may think that their position as manager will be undermined by allowing others to show the way. The reverse is true. If a manager prevents others from showing the way, and cannot themselves show the way, not only will the team lack direction but others will not learn to show leadership. All that it takes is for a jealous manager to bite someone's head off when they attempt to show the way. The person concerned is unlikely to try to lead again, and others will take note and not offer suggestions and ideas. Thomas Sheraton, the furniture designer, understood these issues well. He made his pattern book freely available because he wanted others to learn from him. He knew that not everyone felt the same. "There are men who love to keep their inferiors of the same profession in ignorance that they may have the opportunity of triumphing over them... Their pride will not suffer them to encourage any work which makes others as wise as themselves."[10]

One of the most valuable characteristics in leadership and management is curiosity. The best description of this that I am aware of is from Don Berwick, the paediatrician and renowned leader on quality improvement in health services. Don says:

> It is important that a learning environment be established where it is safe to admit that you do not know. The position of learner is a position of vulnerability and is what we need. To

---

10:    Sheraton, Thomas. *The Cabinet Maker and Upholsterers' Drawing Book* (1793)

willingly place ourselves in the vulnerable position of saying "I do not know how to do this but I have a way to find out." Improvement begins with curiosity and so nurtures an environment in which it is safe to say, "I don't know, let's find out."[11]

The worst sort of managers believe that they have to pretend to know everything and that anything less will be a sign of weakness and will undermine them. The reverse is true. The members of the team know that the manager does not know everything. They do not respect managers who pretend they know everything. They are naturally amused when a manager is found out and it is this ridicule that undermines the manager. If the manager says, "I do not know how to do this; let's find out together," the other members of the team will respect the manager's honesty and will enjoy being part of finding out the answers. Honesty does not make us vulnerable. Honesty makes us strong.

The lives of famous people illustrate these definitions of leadership and management. Let's take three examples: Winston Churchill, Mahatma Gandhi and Nelson Mandela.

Winston Churchill was the first famous person who I became aware of. Although we lived in Myanmar and India until I was twelve, the *Eagle* comic was sent to us. I enjoyed Dan Dare, and all the other characters, but the comic strip that really interested me was one about Churchill. He was portrayed, as he usually is, as the heroic war leader. Later I came to understand that if an aspiring politician had been invited to dine with Churchill in the early thirties, they might have thought twice about it. After the general election of 1929, it was widely assumed that Churchill's long ministerial career, in Liberal and Conservative governments, was over. Churchill was a backbench MP. He did not have command of any resources. He was not a politician-manager. He was not well-regarded. Asquith said of him, "He will never get to the top in English politics, with all his wonderful gifts, to speak with the tongues of men and of angels, and to spend laborious days and nights in administration, is no good, if a man does not inspire trust."[12] But

---

11: Berwick, Don. Speaking at the NHS Top Team meeting (March 2002)

12: Jenkins, Roy. *Churchill: A Biography* (2012)

Churchill began to perform one the most impressive acts of leadership ever shown. He warned the British public about the dangers of the rise of the Nazi party in Germany, at a time when many members of the political and upper classes thought Hitler was to be admired and ought to be accommodated. As early as 19 October 1930 Churchill "was convinced that Hitler or his followers would seize the first opportunity to resort to armed force".[13] For nine years, Churchill showed the way and re-established trust. It was not until September 1939 that he was reappointed to ministerial office as First Lord of the Admiralty and once again became responsible for resources and took up a political role with managerial duties. Churchill was a leader.

Mahatma Gandhi has been in my consciousness for nearly as long as Churchill. Perhaps I heard his name in my early years in India. However, it was not until I chose Indian and African history as my special subjects in my final year at Cambridge that I began to understand what a formidable leader Gandhi was in his early years in South Africa and later in India. Gandhi had no wish to be responsible for resources; he had no desire to be a politician-manager, to be the first prime minister of an independent India. However, through his simple and powerful words and acts, he showed the way to his people; he showed that they could make it impossible for the British to continue to rule India, that India could, and would, be free. The greatest empire of modern times had to give up its most valued possession. It was Jawaharlal Nehru who would become both leader and manager, the first prime minister of independent India. It was Gandhi who showed the way, though. His words will always challenge would-be leaders: "If we could change ourselves, the tendencies in the world would also change. As a man changes his own nature, so does the attitude of the world change towards him." This was later adapted into the famous quotation: "You must be the change you want to see in the world."[14]

Nelson Mandela was a towering figure of the modern world. I began to support the Labour Party during my time at Cambridge, from 1966 to 1969. Mandela had been arrested in 1962 and tried in 1963–4 and

13:    Gilbert, Martin. *Winston S. Churchill, Volume V, Part 2: Documents: The Wilderness Years 1929–1935* (2009)

14:    Gandhi, Mahatma. *The Collected Works, Vol XII* (1964)

was in prison for twenty-seven years. Support for Mandela and the anti-apartheid movement was an article of faith for many young people. In all the years in prison, Nelson Mandela was not a politician-manager. He had no responsibility for the use of resources. However, for all that time, and for the many years he was confined to a small cell with a bucket for a toilet and forced to do hard labour, Mandela showed the way because he kept alive the belief that one day South Africa would be a multiracial democracy. Mandela achieved this even though his words and image were banned. He was a leader long before he became president of his country and assumed responsibility for its resources as a politician-manager.

We can also see my definitions of leadership and management – leadership is showing the way and management is the responsibility for the use of resources – were illustrated every day in the work of teams. It is easy to see who the manager is. They have the title and the role. They are responsible for the use of resources. It may be more difficult to see who the leaders are. It may be that the manager is also a leader, showing the way to the team. It may be that the manager is not a leader but has the grace and good sense to allow others to lead. It may be that the manager is not able to lead and discourages others from showing the way because they feel threatened.

Understanding what leadership and management are is the first step in developing as a leader and a manager. Once this is understood, it is possible to move on to think about the values and behaviours that encourage leadership and management to flourish.

One other point about leadership: it is often assumed that leadership is a *good thing*. Leadership is showing the way. Whether it is a good thing or not depends on whether the way being shown is a *good* way. That will depend on the match between your values and beliefs and the direction of travel. Leadership is not necessarily a good thing. The same ethical standards must be applied to leadership as to anything else. History is full of leaders who have led their followers to evil and destruction. However, they were leaders because they showed the way, even if it was the wrong way.

Of course, knowledge of your work, professional and technical expertise, and experience are all important in building credibility in leadership and management. However, values and behaviour are vital. What we do and what we say, what we believe and who we are, have a huge impact on our effectiveness as leaders and managers and on those we manage and aspire to lead. This is often ignored or underplayed in discussions on leadership and management. This may be because it is very challenging to realise that every single thing we do and say, what we believe and who we are, impacts on our credibility and on others. It is so much easier to rely on qualifications, knowledge or experience. However, qualifications, knowledge and experience will only take us so far. If we want to grow as leaders and managers, if we want to serve, then we have to be willing to reflect on our behaviour and to learn the values and behaviours that will enable us to flourish.

Here are the first six of the 40 questions to consider before we move on to think about why leadership and management are important. Rennie Fritchie, who was the second chair I worked with at the Gloucester Health Authority and from whom I learned a great deal, suggested that it would be a good idea to answer these questions in dialogue with a colleague who you respect and trust. This seems to me a good idea.

1. What are your definitions of leadership and management, and do your definitions help you to grow as a leader and manager?
2. Can you think of people you have known who were leaders even though they were not managers?
3. Can you think of managers you have worked with who were also leaders?
4. Can you think of managers who were not leaders but encouraged leadership in others?
5. Can you think of managers who could not lead themselves but discouraged leadership from others because they felt threatened?
6. Reflecting on your own experience, which of these situations worked best in terms of the well-being of the team and the team's effectiveness in getting things done?

Chapter Two

Why Are Leadership and Management Important?

For much of my time as a manager, and as someone aspiring to leadership, I had to believe that leadership and management were important! For many years, it was an article of faith. I had no doubt at all that the organisation I had the privilege of serving – the National Health Service – was important. The evidence was there every day for me to see. People being cared for, treated and cured. Lives saved and life chances enhanced. However, I did not have objective evidence that what I did made a difference. I knew that if I behaved well towards people, they were happier and more likely to get things done. I knew that issues were resolved because of the work I did and that the work of the front-line staff was made easier when I was able to deal with the issues they brought to me. Later in my career I knew it gave me great satisfaction to see that services sometimes improved because I was able to allocate additional resources and to plan services that were more effective and patient-centred. Many people, particularly when I was leaving jobs, were very generous in their comments about the difference I had made to their well-being and work. All of this I knew.

I began to understand that real change came from four things:

- having a clear view about what you want to achieve
- developing people to their maximum capacity
- making processes as effective and efficient as possible
- deploying resources effectively

I was often confronted with organisational change, and indeed, did a fair bit of it myself. However, I came to understand that organisational change rarely produces real change. Indeed, it is sometimes adopted as a means of avoiding real issues. One example of this is when a manager is not functioning effectively. It is not easy to deal with poor performance. It requires courage, preparation, sensitivity and resilience. (Appraisal and feedback are discussed in more detail in Chapter Five.) Rather than addressing performance it is much easier to reorganise the structure. If the poorly-performing manager is one of a number at a level of management, it is much simpler to reduce the number of posts at that level, go through an appointments process, and not appoint the poorly-performing manager to one of the new posts.

At a higher level, merging organisations is a favoured pastime and is sometimes preferred to tackling poorly-performing organisations. Those tempted by this solution – which is sometimes necessary and appropriate – should first read the report from the King's Fund that concludes that mergers rarely achieve the stated objectives.[15] One example of this is the attempt to integrate health and social care services. It is sometimes claimed that integration has been achieved simply by transferring staff from one service to another. Nothing is further from the truth! Transferring staff is only the first step. If integrated services are to be effective that can only be achieved by:

- a clear sense of shared purpose
- intensive training for new roles and extensive organisational development with a focus on team working
- reviewing processes in detail to reduce duplication and ensure that staff from the different backgrounds are following the same procedures and that the new procedures are supporting integration
- redeploying resources between services and teams to ensure that the highest priorities are being addressed

15:     Collins, Ben. 'Foundation Trust and NHS Trust Mergers', Kings Fund (2015)

I also learned that there are seven ingredients in performance management.

Clarity about the objectives: If you are not clear about what you are trying to achieve, there is little hope of improved performance. Rennie Fritchie helped me to understand the difference between the urgent and the important, and this is particularly useful when setting objectives. Ruthless and frequent prioritisation is essential in setting objectives. It will always be helpful to ask yourself if the objective is urgent, important or both. The urgent issues need to be tackled first but the important issues need to stay on the list. If there is more than one urgent objective, and there almost always is, rank the urgent objectives in order of importance. Give priority to deadlines that are set for you rather than deadlines over which you have control yourself. Often when I have been working with a client as a coach they have identified the number of deadlines they were facing as a major source of stress. I always ask them to distinguish between the deadlines that are set for them and the deadlines over which they have control. They often find, to their surprise, that at least some of the stress comes from deadlines they have set for themselves. These can easily be reset, particularly if you remember to distinguish between the urgent and the important.

Commitment to delivery: The will to do it. If the person managing and/or leading the project is not committed to delivery, there is little chance that the rest of the team, on whom achievement will depend, will be committed.

Capacity to deliver: Are the resources available to achieve the objectives? Have too many objectives been set for the capacity available?

Evidence of progress: Good-quality information. If you do not have reliable and timely evidence you will not know how you are doing and will not be able to change your approach to deal with the issues that are slowing or preventing progress.

Rigour: Effective monitoring and holding to account. It is not enough to have the information; it must be rigorously interrogated and progress must be constantly monitored. Everyone involved must hold themselves and others to account.

Resilience and staying power: Everyone faces setbacks and disappointments. In fact, if everything is going smoothly, you are right to be suspicious. It may be that you are not being told the truth. You need to value the people who bring you the bad news, as John Harvey Jones' says.[16] Doing the right thing is always difficult. Very few worthwhile things are achieved easily. If you believe that you are doing the right thing, you must find the resilience and staying power to keep trying.

Getting the best from the most important resource: The people you are managing and aspiring to lead. That can only be done by good management and leadership.

The link between achieving real change and performance management is the people. You will only achieve real change and improve performance if you get the best from the people on whom your success will always depend. As James Beier said, "No matter how much an executive knew about the technical side, he had to get things done through people."[17] Peter Drucker said that Greenleaf "was always out to change the individual".[18]

I learned all this the hard way, so I knew that leadership and management were important and made a difference to people's well-being, their effectiveness and the achievement of objectives. However, it was not until much later in my career, that the research-based evidence became available as a result of the work of Beverly Alimo-Metcalfe, Michael West and others.

The first piece of research that really had an impact on me and provided me with evidence of the importance of leadership and management was the work done by Carol Borrill and colleagues including Michael West from the Institute of Work Psychology in Sheffield.[19] They studied the mental health of 12,000 staff in nineteen NHS trusts. Their

---

16:    Harvey-Jones, John. *Making it Happen* (1988)

17:    Beier, James. *The Earlhamite*, July 1967, quoted in Frick. Op. cit.

18:    Drucker, Peter. Introduction to *On Becoming a Servant Leader: The Private Writings of Robert K. Greenleaf* (Frick, Don M. and Spears, Larry C., eds) (1996)

19:    Borrill, C. S. et al. 'Stress Among Staff in NHS Trusts Final Report', Institute of Work Psychology, University of Sheffield and Psychological Therapies Research Centre, University of Leeds (1998)

disturbing conclusion was that the mental health of NHS staff was worse than that of the employed population as a whole. The researchers identified seven "constructs" that explained the situation:

- work demands – having too much work to do
- role ambiguity – confusion over who should do what
- role conflict – hard-pressed staff arguing about who should do what
- lack of social support – staff feeling that they were not supported by their colleagues
- lack of influence over decisions – staff not included in decision-making about their work
- professional compromise – the uncomfortable awareness that they were not caring for and treating patients in the way they knew the patients ought to be treated

What struck me about these conclusions was how many of the constructs were influenced by management and leadership. Managers are responsible for the use of resources. People are their most important resource. It is the responsibility of managers to help staff to cope with work demands through the fair allocation of work and the appropriate deployment of resources. It is the job of managers to make clear what is expected of staff and to ensure tasks and responsibilities are clearly allocated. Managers have the opportunity, through their own behaviour and by setting an example, to make sure that staff feel supported. Managers can ensure that staff have appropriate influence over their work. It is important that managers are aware of professional compromise, do all they can to prevent it and to support staff in coping with it when it occurs. Here for me was clear evidence that leadership and management are important and that the quality of leadership and management directly affects the mental health of staff, a major factor in their well-being and effectiveness.

Another fascinating piece of research was that done by Michael West and his colleagues on the management of employees and patient mortality. The research "demonstrated strong links between human resources practices and patient mortality in hospitals. It has suggested that it may be possible to significantly influence hospital performance by implementing sophisticated and extensive training and appraisal systems, and encouraging a high percentage of employees to work in teams."[20]

Beverly Alimo-Metcalfe has been one of the greatest influences on my thinking about leadership and management and on my attempts to lead and manage. Beverly conducted a major study of 700 mental health teams. The conclusion of this important research was that "[a] high quality of leadership and management is positively associated with positive staff attitudes to work, their well-being at work and with the achievement of organisational goals".[21]

Staff who were well-led and managed were more positive about their work, happier and healthier at work and got things done.

The research, and Beverly's work on engaging leadership, are discussed in Chapter Four.

Michael West's research on effective teams concluded that effective teams deliver better patient satisfaction, performance and morale.[22] According to Michael West, effective teams have:

- clear identity and purpose
- clear, agreed team objectives
- role clarity
- effective communication
- appropriate involvement in decision-making
- constructive debate
- good inter-team working
- regular meetings to review performance and adapt appropriately

All of these things will be influenced by the quality of management and leadership in the team. If the team has effective management and

20:    West, M. A. et al. 'The link between the management of employees and patient mortality in acute hospitals'. *The International Journal of Human Resource Management,* 13, 8, 1299–1310 (2002)

21:    Alimo-Metcalfe et al. 'The impact of engaging leadership on performance, attitudes to work and well-being at work: a longitudinal study'. *Journal of Health and Organizational Management,* vol 22 (2008)

22:    West, M. *Effective Teamwork* (2012)

a manager who understands leadership and encourages it to flourish, these characteristics are more likely to be present. Leadership and management make a difference.

In 2013 the results of a study by Mary Dixon Woods, Michael West and their colleagues, was published in the *BMJ*.[23] The study concluded that good staff support and management were highly variable, though they were fundamental to culture and directly related to patient experience, safety and the quality of care. Clear, challenging goals were important. Organisations needed to put the patient at the centre of everything they do. They also needed to get useful intelligence, to focus on improving organisational systems and to nurture caring cultures by ensuring that staff feel valued, respected, engaged and supported.

Once again all of these characteristics of an organisation are more likely to be present if an organisation has effective leadership and management.

23:    Dixon-Woods, M. et al. Culture and behaviour in the English NHS. *British Medical Journal* (2013)

Chapter Three

Human Nature

Leadership and management are about getting the best out of people. It makes sense, therefore, to think about human nature. As with everything else it is important to be realistic and to see human nature as it is and not as we would like it to be. Human beings are capable of everything and run the spectrum from Gandhi and Nelson Mandela to Hitler. In my life, and in my many years of public service, I have encountered behaviour at both extremes. The vast majority of people I have worked with and encountered in my personal life are genuine, hardworking, and trustworthy. The very best have been capable of acts of great kindness, compassion and generosity. The world of health and social care, in which I have spent the majority of my working life, attracts some people of extraordinary intellect, expertise and self-sacrifice. I have seen and experienced human nature at its best.

However, I have also seen human nature at close to its worst. I have seen carelessness, laziness, indifference, cruelty, jealously, untrustworthiness, dishonesty and selfishness.

If you aspire to lead and to manage, it is important to be realistic about human nature. Certainly it is good to look for the best, but it is also wise to expect the worst. One example of this, which I experienced very early on, was colleagues resisting changes in working practice on the grounds that the changes were not in the patients' best interests. Of course, it is very important for managers to listen very carefully to colleagues who care directly for patients and service users and who are concerned for their welfare. However, I soon discovered that I needed to thoroughly check the facts. If I was convinced that patients would suffer, if I could find evidence to support the claim, I was always keen to reconsider and see what could be done to limit or remove the harm. There were cases where it became clear that colleagues were using the patients' best interests to disguise their own! The real reason they were opposed to change was because they realised that the changes would lead to more work for them or inconvenient working hours or would ask more of them than they were willing to give. Far from championing the interest of patients, they were defending their own interests.

Another example is the way in which managers behaved towards members of their team who had great potential. The best of human nature was on display when managers did all they could to encourage and support the development of their colleagues even to the point where the colleague found greater success than the manager themselves had experienced. The worst was there to be seen when managers did everything they could to limit the development of their colleagues because their primary interest was in preserving their own position. They were motivated by jealousy and self-protection. They cared nothing for the talent of their colleagues or the benefit to customers that would flow from fully-developed expertise. They were only concerned for themselves. Selfishness and jealousy can destroy careers and well-being at work.

A further example is the way in which managers behave when something goes wrong and whether or not they support their staff. This issue is discussed in Chapter Five.

A realistic view of human nature is also of great importance when dealing with poor performance by staff. The most important thing is to try and find out why the performance is poor. Is the person concerned incapable of doing the job? Do they lack the necessary intelligence, skills or experience? A manager who aspires to fairness and support will do all they can to remedy the deficiency with training, coaching or supervised experience. A manager who cares nothing for the people they work with will not care why the poor performance is occurring but will blame, discipline and drive the member of staff out at the earliest opportunity. If it is clear that the poor performance is the result of laziness, indifference or lack of effort, the person concerned needs to be managed ever more closely, disciplined and ultimately dismissed. The NHS does not exist to provide jobs although it does the country a great service, particularly in struggling areas, by doing just that. The

NHS exists to serve patients, and lazy or indifferent staff harm patient care. They need to be dealt with both for the sake of patients and also for the sake of conscientious staff who may well have to do extra work because of the poor performance of their colleagues.

What happened

When I was deputy superintendent at the Royal Hospital in Sheffield I discovered that one of the things the surgical ward sisters worried about was the fact that one of our surgical barbers who shaved patients before operations – a job now done by support workers – drank alcohol at lunchtime. This resulted in hands that trembled and the sisters were understandably concerned about the potential damage to delicate parts of the body! I waited in the joiners' shop, which was on the corner of the site near the entrance the barber used to return to the hospital. I spoke to the barber, and he smelled of alcohol. He was dismissed.

What I learned

Patients come first. If a member of staff is behaving in a way that compromises patients' safety, the situation needs to be dealt with urgently and effectively. The barber was putting his consumption of alcohol before patient safety. Selfish behaviour puts people at risk. I also learned the importance of listening to concerns expressed by staff. The sisters were concerned and I listened.

What happened

When I was sector administrator of the Nottingham General and University Hospitals the only operational service that I was responsible for was the porters. Everything else was managed from the district headquarters. I discovered that there was a lot of one-day sickness, which is the kind of absence managers should be most concerned about. If someone is off sick for a long period because of a serious illness, that is very sad for them and those that love them and may cause staffing problems. However, the manager does not need to worry about whether the individual is behaving well or not. The cause of the absence is clear. It is when people have a lot of one-day sickness that the manager needs to worry. One-day sickness may occur not because people are unwell but because they would rather be doing something else instead of working – watching a football match, going fishing, playing golf, going shopping or simply adding time off to a weekend or bank holiday, or recovering from the effects of having had too much of a good time!

I was very young at the time, only twenty-eight. Trade unions in the 1970s had a great deal of power and could be militant. The shop stewards were considerably older and more experienced than I was. I arranged to see the shop stewards to discuss the one-day sickness, and I was very nervous. It would have been very embarrassing if the only operational service I was responsible for went out on strike. To my relief, the shop stewards welcomed the discussion and were keen to work with me to tackle the problem. It turned out that their conscientious members were fed up of being called in to work on their rest days to cover for sickness which they knew, or strongly suspected, had nothing to do with sickness and everything to do with laziness or prioritising leisure over work. We began to talk to the individuals with the worst records and pointed out any patterns that appeared to suggest planned absence rather than genuine sickness. Simply talking to people made a difference because they realised they had been rumbled. If there was no improvement, we followed the normal practice of referrals to occupational health followed by disciplinary action. Things got better, and fewer conscientious staff had their days off disturbed.

What I learned

Human nature ranges from the best to the worst. Although most people would only take time off when they were genuinely ill there were those who took time off because they were lazy or preferred to be paid for enjoying themselves. Conscientious staff, the ones displaying human nature at its best, were glad to see those behaving badly dealt with firmly but fairly. Services improved and there was less strain on those who behaved well. Trade unions and staff will support managers who act fairly to deal with laziness and indifference.

What happened

I appointed a senior colleague, who turned out to be one of the laziest people I have ever met. Laziness is very difficult to detect in a selection process. Even lazy people make an effort if they want to get a job! The person appointed did really well in the interview and was fluent and persuasive. They had an impressive CV with all the right qualifications and experience. It was only when they started the job that it became clear that they were lazy and had no intention of making any reasonable effort to do the well-paid job. Once the best possible lease car had been obtained and an attractive office in one of our nicer buildings had been allocated to them, they lost all interest. The only way to deal with this, having carried out a realistic assessment of the causes of the poor performance, was to manage the person ever more closely and, eventually, out of the organisation!

What I learned

Laziness is very difficult to detect in selection procedure. Laziness is one of the least attractive aspects of human nature. There is not much you can do about it. No amount of training, coaching or supervised practice will turn a lazy person into a conscientious person. Manage them closely, and probably out!

And now to the next five of the 40 questions to think about before we go on to consider the values and behaviours needed for leadership.

7.   Do you have a realistic view of human nature?
8.   Do you look for the best but expect the worst also?
9.   When things go badly wrong, do you display the worst of human nature by leaving your staff to their fate or do you show the best of human nature by supporting them and being on their side while fully cooperating in the investigation and any necessary disciplinary action?
10.   When performance is poor, do you assess the causes carefully, providing support, training, coaching and

supervised practice where the cause is a lack of experience or expertise, and dealing firmly and fairly with the individual if the cause is laziness or indifference?

11.   Do you put customers and conscientious staff first by dealing with the staff who are not delivering?

As well as thinking about human nature in general terms it is vital to understand ourselves and each other. Aristotle said, "Knowing yourself is the beginning of all wisdom."[24]

What happened

In Chapter Five I explain that in 1991, at the age of forty-three, I faced a formidable combination of work pressures and personal problems and that the personal problems related to the fact that I was beginning to understand myself and to face up to who I was. In common with many men I had been carried along through school, university, work and a family life without really understanding who I was. This led me to seek help from a psychotherapist, and later, to many years of counselling. At the same time, I began to work with a coach, Bob Dearden, and continued to work with him until I retired from full-time work in 2005. Bob's wisdom, experience and challenge were extremely valuable to me and I don't think I would have survived in senior roles as long as I did without his support. One of the many good things Bob did for me was to arrange for me to be introduced to Myers–Briggs.[25] The indicator was administered and expertly explained to me by Jocelyn Ryder Smith. Not everyone has a good experience of Myers–Briggs. Sometimes the instrument is administered, and feedback received, online, with little explanation of the origins and meaning of the approach. People also sometimes feel pressured into agreeing with what personality type they are. I was lucky!

24:    Aristotle, Nicomachean. *Ethics* (349 BC)

25:    Myers–Briggs. The Indicator, OPP Ltd

What I learned

I became fascinated by the people who had produced the Myers–Briggs Type Indicator (MBTI). and learned a great deal about myself. I found that the psychological type that was the best fit for me was INFJ – introverted intuition with extroverted feeling. I began to understand that I had a strong preference for introversion and that the orientation of my energy was directed internally to my inner world, reflecting on thoughts, memories and feelings. The extroverted behaviour that I displayed much of the time in the working environment, including public speaking, was learned behaviour and took a great deal out of me. I needed time to be alone to recover and recharge. I understood that I preferred to take in information by intuition, seeing the big picture and focusing on the relationships and connections between facts. I also learned that I had to make a special effort to see the practical realities. I realised that I made my decisions with reference to feelings and values, considering what was important to me and to others and exercising empathy. I learned that I needed to make a special effort to base decisions on evidence as well as values. I understood that I preferred to deal with the external world in a planned and orderly way and that sticking to plans is very important to me. I still struggle with flexibility and spontaneity!

Because I found the Myers–Briggs approach so helpful I have used it in my own life and attended the excellent training programme organised by OPP to use Myers–Briggs in working with others, both for individual coaching and in team development.[26]

Whenever I am using Myers–Briggs I begin with the story of the remarkable women who developed the system. It all began in 1917 when Katherine C. Briggs began to study individual difference through biography. In 1923 Jung's *Psychological Types* was translated into English, and for eighteen years Katherine and her daughter, Isabel Briggs Myers, studied Jung's theory and observed personality in terms of type. America's entry in to World War II in 1941 prompted them to develop the indicator in order "to do something that might help peoples understand

---

26:    OPP Ltd. Op. cit.

each other and avoid destructive conflict".[27] The research and development of the indicator continued over many years. Katherine and Isabel had many useful contacts. Katherine's husband, and Isabel's Father, was Lyman Briggs who became director of the National Bureau of Standards in the USA during the Great Depression. Isabel apprenticed herself to Edward N. Hay, who founded the Hay Consultancy, now one of the largest management consultancy firms in the world.

The indicator did not become widely available until 1975. If you want to understand the Myers–Briggs approach, there is no substitute for reading *Gifts Differing: Understanding Personality Type* by Isabel and her son Peter B. Myers.[27] It was published in 1980, the year of Isabel's death. I love the fact that the book was not published until sixty-three years after Katherine began her studies. This tells us that important work is rarely quick or easy. It takes time, resilience and determination. The book is dedicated to "all who desire to make fuller use of their gifts" and begins with St Paul's reminder in Romans 12 that we all have "gifts differing".[28]

Katherine and Isabel would have been appalled that the process is sometimes reduced to an online report and that people are simply told which personality type they are. Their only concern was that people should understand themselves and others better. *Introduction to Type*, written by Isabel, suggested a three-step process.[29] First a self-estimate based on listening to, or reading, the descriptions of type. Second the reported type based on the choices made in completing the indicator. The third and crucial stage is the process of selecting your "best fit" type based on studying the sixteen type descriptions. Katherine and Isabel would have had no problem with people changing their "best fit" type as their understanding of themselves developed.

When we understand ourselves, we can then try to be true to ourselves. We can appreciate our strengths and our needs and learn to compensate for our weaknesses. Know yourself and be true to yourself.

When I gave my presidential address to the Institute of Health Services Management in 1985 I noted that the address was "a personal

---

27:　Briggs-Myers, Isabel. *Gifts Differing: Understanding Personality Types* (1980)

28:　St Paul. Romans 12:6

29:　Briggs-Myers, Isabel. *Introduction to Type: A Guide to Understanding Your Results on the MBTI Indictor* (1980)

statement. This might seem to free the president from all constraints. And yet nothing is more constraining than speaking for yourself. When you speak for yourself, it is vital to be true to yourself. I know of no harsher or more worthwhile discipline."[30]

Being true to yourself is difficult and demands courage and resilience.

It is also vital to look after yourself and to be kind to yourself. As Theodore Isaac Rubin said: "Compassion for myself is the most powerful healer of all."[31]

Here are three more questions for reflection:

12. Do you understand yourself?
13. Have you used Myers–Briggs or other approaches to help you to understand yourself and others?
14. Are you true to yourself?

30:    Jarrold, Ken. Presidential Address at Hospital and Health Services Review (1985)

31:    Rubin, Isaac Theodore. *Compassion and Self Hate* (1975)

Chapter Four

The Values and Behaviours Needed for Leadership

Many of the values and behaviours needed for management are also needed for leadership. However, there are some behaviours that are particularly helpful if we are to learn to lead and serve.

It is only possible to learn and adopt these behaviours if we start by understanding what leadership is. Once we understand the definition discussed in Chapter One then we have a foundation on which to build the required behaviours. So we begin by understanding that leadership is showing the way.

In his book *What Leaders Really Do*, John Kotter, whose thinking has influenced me greatly, discussed the importance of "core behaviour".

> The central issue here is not one of style. I often hear people say that we need a "new leadership style" for the new century. In a globalising world with a better educated workforce that is no longer inclined to be seen and not heard, a new leadership is in fact called for, but style is not the key leadership issue. Substance is. It is about core behaviour on the job, not the surface details and tactics, a core that changes little over time, across different cultures, or in different industries.[32]

There are four behaviours that are helpful if we are to learn to lead and serve.

32:   Kotter, John P. *What Leaders Really Do* (1999)

The first behaviour required is having the courage to show the way. This is particularly important if you are in a role from which leadership would not be expected. Understanding that leadership is showing the way and is not dependent on having a management role is the beginning. If you understand this, it will give you the awareness that you too can lead. It does not matter how junior or inexperienced you are. If you know the way you can show the way. Courage is "the ability to do something that frightens one."[33] It is right to be frightened about showing the way, providing leadership, because there will always be those who resent others showing the way, particularly if the person is junior or inexperienced. There will always be people who are threatened by leadership when it is shown by others. They cannot accept that someone else can provide leadership. They may believe that their position or reputation will be threatened by someone else showing the way. Awareness of these less attractive aspects of human nature should not put us off from providing leadership. If we do not have the courage to show the way, we will keep quiet and people will not have the opportunity to consider the direction we are suggesting. I have known brilliant and experienced and even senior people who simply did not have the courage to show the way. Even though they knew the way, they were afraid of the reaction they might receive. They feared loss of face or ridicule. Courage is fundamental to leadership.

David Wilkinson and Elaine Appleby in their excellent book, *Implementing Holistic Government*, for which they kindly asked me to write the foreword, say that "courage is probably more appropriate than charisma".[34] That has been my experience. What is the point of high-gloss presentation skills if you do not have the courage to show the way? You can be the most beguiling and charming person but fail your colleagues and the people you serve because you do not have courage. There is no point in knowing what to do if you do not have the courage to show the way to others. Julian Hartley, one of the most effective and able chief executives in the NHS, says that "leadership

---

33:   *Oxford English Dictionary*

34:   Wilkinson, David and Applebee Canon, Elaine. Implementing Holistic Government – Joined up action on the ground. Policy Press, Bristol (1999)

is about character and courage".[35] Peter Ackroyd, in his biography of Thomas Moore, says Martin Luther "possessed the authentic voice of the free and separate conscience and somehow found the power to stand against the world he had inherited".[36] Courage is the power to stand against. As C. S. Lewis remanded us, "Courage is not simply one of the virtues but the form of every virtue at the testing point, which means at the point of highest reality."[37]

Greenleaf was clear that leaders need to be willing to challenge:

> In the nature of any institution is compromise. And a fatal error for a leader is to see his role largely as the mediator of compromise, the keeper of the peace. Clearly, he must do some of this, but there is a larger role to excite the institution with demanding goals; larger goals than the machinery of compromise would postulate. The larger role means reaching to make the impossible possible, insistently demanding it at times, and venturing to challenge mediocrity.[38]

Courage comes in many forms. One of my favourite types of courage is courageous patience – having the patience to wait for the right time to see things through with courage. Mary Anne Radmacher reminds us that "courage does not always roar. Sometimes courage is that little voice at the end of the day that says, 'I'll try again tomorrow.'"[39] Courage is often associated with dramatic action. Alan Bennett warns us about the quiet moments: "The majority of people perform well in a crisis and when the spotlight is on them; it's on the Sunday afternoons of this life, when nobody is looking, that the spirit falters."[40] Simon Caulkin, who writes for the *Guardian* and *Observer*, made this point very well when he

35:   Hartley, Julian. Leadership in the NHS: Connecting for the Future. Geoff Scaife Memorial Lecture. NHS Confederation (2005)

36:   Ackroyd, Peter. *The Life of Thomas Moore, Chatto and Windus* (1991)

37:   Lewis C. S. *The Screwtape Letters* (1942)

38:   Greenleaf, R. K. *The Servant As Leader* (1970)

39:   Radmacher, Mary Anne. *Lean Forward into Your Life* (2007)

40:   Bennett, Alan. *Writing Home* (1994)

said, "Good management is not about cleverness or number-crunching ability. It is about individual honesty and courage and a willingness to worry a way through the hard decisions."[41]

The second behaviour required for leadership is to clearly and simply explain what needs to be done. Sometimes a person will know the way but be unable to explain it. This may be because they do not understand the virtues of simplicity, or it may be because they mistakenly believe that complexity and mystery give an impression of cleverness and intellect. My experience is that it takes more intellectual ability to explain things simply than to do so at great length. It is much harder to write a short piece than to ramble on endlessly. Many of the most influential statements ever made have been short and simple:

- Lord's Prayer: 79 words
- Sermon on the Mount: 143 words
- Ten Commandments: 173 words
- Gettysburg Address: 286 words
- United States Declaration of Independence: 1,322 words

We need to understand that simplicity is not a matter of shame and that complexity is not an indication of brilliance.

People respond to short, simple, understandable statements. Short, simple, understandable stories are particularly effective. Alan Langlands, former chief executive of the NHS in England, for whom I deputised on general management issues during my time as director of human resources from 1994–97, said, "The best leaders have also developed... the power of synthesis and they are good at telling stories."[42] The objective in showing the way is not to show how clever we are. The objective is to explain things in a way that people can understand and follow.

The third required behaviour is to persuade people to follow. Of course, there are situations in which there is no time to persuade, in which clear instructions have to be given. This is certainly true in

---

41:    Caulkin, Simon. The Guardian

42:    Langlands, Alan. Edited Kath Aspinall. A View from Here: Personal Perspective on the Future of the NHS. York Symposium on Health (1996)

emergency health situations or in situations of danger such as armed conflict. However, in the vast majority of situations there is time to persuade. The definition in the Cambridge Dictionary is helpful: "To make someone do or believe something by giving them a good reason to do it or talking to that person and making them believe it."[43] Robert Greenleaf used a wonderful Quaker term to describe the desired result of persuasion: "convincement". He said, "Leadership by persuasion has the virtue of change by convincement rather than coercion."[44] That is, getting to the point where the people you are aspiring to lead are convinced for themselves.

Rennie Fritchie describes the strategy most likely to lead to convincement. Some people try to convince you by "selling" their answer and trying to push you into their conclusion. Others simply "tell" you the answer without any back up information and they try to direct you to agree with them. Those who "describe" take the time to give the context and background to the information at hand and then work to describe some possibilities and allow you to come to your own conclusions. Describing is much more likely to result in convincement. The beginning of the process is the desire to persuade and that springs from respect for the people you aspire to lead and from the knowledge that people who are convinced for themselves will make a much better job of following.

Some people, often those who assume that they have a right to lead because of their role and seniority, do not understand the need for persuasion. They believe that they have a right to show the way and a right to assume that people will follow. Both assumptions are wrong. No one has the right to lead because of their position. Only people who can show the way have the right to lead and they should do their best to take people with them. This is where we begin to understand the values that underpin servant leadership and management. Respect for colleagues of all seniorities and roles is crucial. We should treat people the same whoever they are and whatever they do. If we try to live by that value, then persuasion is an obvious behaviour.

43:    *Cambridge Dictionary*

44:    Greenleaf, R. K. *The Servant As Leader* (1970)

The fourth behaviour that is required is enabling others to lead if you do not know the way yourself. Jealousy is a common and destructive emotional response to other people showing the way. Some people find it difficult to accept that someone else has had a good idea and is showing the way. They wish they had thought of it first. They think they should be the leader because they are older, more senior or more experienced. They cannot bear to see someone else get the credit for leadership. They would rather the way was not shown than it was shown by someone else. They would prefer the team to go in the wrong direction under their leadership rather than in the right direction under someone else's leadership. Human nature can be ugly and jealousy is one of its least lovely features. However, if we can find the grace to accept leadership from others, it can be intensely liberating for us and for those around us. It is particularly powerful if the manager, someone in a senior role or a very experienced person, accepts leadership from someone more junior or less experienced. If the manager says to the rest of the team that they believe the way being shown by someone else is the way to go and that they intend to support and enable the direction, that is very powerful. Managers who find the grace and humility to follow leadership from others will not weaken their position. They will be admired and respected.

A crucial factor is how we respond to ideas put forward by others. If we respond negatively to attempts by others to show the way, we will discourage them from showing the way. Even if they seem to be wrong this time, they may be right next time. However, there will not be a next time if they feel reluctant to express their ideas. If they feel humiliated by sarcastic and negative responses, they will not share their thoughts and ideas. We may also make the mistake of not properly considering the way being proposed because of the person who is showing the way. We may dismiss their proposal because we do not value or respect them. We may think they are foolish or stupid or unreliable. They may be all of those things but they might be right about the issue they are addressing. Leadership can and does come from people who are not often right!

What happened

Over the years, I have taken a particular interest in services for people with learning disabilities. This began when I saw how young men with a learning disability were treated at the hospital to which I was attached as a trainee in 1970. It was regarded as one of the more progressive hospitals, but I was appalled by what I saw. The young men were treated like animals with no respect for their dignity or privacy. I was struck by the contrast between the privileged life I had been leading at Cambridge, with all the comforts of an ancient college, and the way in which these men of my own age were being treated only a few miles away.

Over the years, as I had the privilege to be involved in the provision of better services, particularly in Gloucester and Durham, I had the opportunity to observe the interaction between the people being cared for and the people who cared for them. I began to understand that the most effective leadership in the care of an individual was given by the person who knew the resident best. It was not a matter of seniority, long service or qualifications; it was about who knew the resident best. It was about who understood what they liked and did not like, who understood their moods and knew the signs that challenging behaviour was about to happen. A wise ward sister or home manager would listen to a support worker who knew a resident well and could see trouble was around the corner. An unwise manager would dismiss the advice because it came from a support worker and they felt that they knew best because of their qualifications and position.

What I learned

I learned that leadership is not a matter of role or position. Leadership is about knowing the way and showing the way.

What happened

When I arrived in County Durham and Darlington as the chief executive of the Health Authority in August 1997 I found that the services for people with mental health and learning disabilities were very poor.

The decision had already, rightly, been taken to merge the two small NHS trusts in North and South Durham and to create a single larger trust to cover the whole county and Darlington.

One of the pieces of unfinished business at the Health Authority was the mental health strategy. It seemed important to complete this work in order to provide direction for the new trust. I recruited an able manager to complete the task and, although the draft strategy was far from perfect, I felt it was right to share it with the consultant psychiatrists for discussion. I chaired the meeting myself because I wanted to indicate my strong commitment to these services. I briefly introduced the strategy and invited comments. No one said anything. By this time, I had been working with consultant medical staff for twenty-eight years and I knew that this behaviour was unusual. I found the grace and patience to gently explore what was going on and soon the floodgates of grievance and anger opened. The consultants were completely fed up and demoralised by management that did not listen to them and by a local health service that gave a low priority to the services for people with mental illness and learning disability. Staffing levels were low and recruitment extremely difficult. I might have reacted by asserting my authority and insisting that the strategy was the best way forward. Had I done so I would have alienated them still further and made the journey of recovery and renewal, on which we were soon to embark, much more difficult. Instead I found the wisdom and grace to say, "OK. I will withdraw the strategy and start again with your full involvement." The mood of the meeting changed immediately. The consultants were surprised and even shocked by my response. There was still a great deal of suspicion and it would be many months before they trusted me, but it was a start. I invited them to nominate one consultant from the north and one from the south to work with me and the new chief executive of the trust, meeting in my office to put together a new approach. A wonderful process of recovery and renewal followed, with substantial investment in staffing and new buildings. When I retired in 2005, I received a wonderful letter from one of the consultants who had been nominated to work with us. He said, "I well remember going into your office on a sunny Friday in September... I am not sure that at that time I realistically expected to achieve anything, but without your vision and leadership I am sure that services would not have developed as they have done... It really is truly astonishing the transformation that has taken place in seven years."

What I learned

Leadership involves listening and respect for the people you are aspiring to lead. You cannot lead effectively by throwing your weight about and insisting that your approach is right. You need to listen and build trust over time. You need to share the task of leadership, you need to work with others to show the way. You are not the leader because you are the chief executive. If you are the chief executive you can lead if you listen and work with those who know the way.

It's time for three more of our 40 questions to consider before we move on to think about the values and behaviours needed for management

15. Do the four behaviours described here make sense to you based on your experience of leading and being led?
    · courage
    · clearly and simply explaining what needs to be done
    · persuading others to follow
    · enabling others to lead
16. Have you observed other behaviours that enhance or undermine leadership?
17. If you agree that the behaviours described here are desirable, how easy have you found it to behave in this way when you have aspired to leadership?

Chapter Five

The Values and Behaviours Needed for Management

Many of the values and behaviours needed for leadership are also relevant to management. What matters is what you say, what you do and how you behave. What we do and how we behave is strongly influenced by our values.

Here we will consider values and behaviours in relation to management using the definition suggested in Chapter One. Management is the responsibility for the use of resources. Management is dependent on role and seniority.

Most organisations have four levels of managers:

- team managers
- senior managers, usually responsible for a number of team managers
- directors, often members of a management, executive team or board
- chief executives

In my experience the most important level of management is the team managers. It is the team managers who impact directly on the quality and effectiveness of the work done by the team and on the well-being and morale of the staff. As a chief executive, and later as a chair, I was very conscious that we could sit around the board table and think our, sometimes, great thoughts about strategy, policy or resources. We could decide that things should happen. Whether they actually happened was dependent on the individual team managers.

I have observed teams with similar workloads and resources but with very different outcomes in terms of getting things done and cultivating well-motivated staff. The difference was in the quality of the management and leadership in the team. In successful teams the staff wanted to come to work and were committed to what they did and to each other. In less successful teams, sickness and absence levels were high, there was a lack of commitment to the work, and a lack of support for colleagues.

Robert Greenleaf describes team managers as being at the interface between the management hierarchy and the frontline staff: "They were the spot where the buck stops. The elaborate executive hierarchy above them thought their great thoughts about what ought to be done. What actually gets done is what these fellows [team managers in RKG's day were usually men] were able, and to some extent willing, to do."[45]

The research by Beverly Alimo-Metcalfe, Michael West and many others suggests that people need four things from their managers.

- support
- feedback, including appraisal
- development and training
- clear job content

My own experience of being managed and of managing others suggests that these are the things that matter.

First, **support**. Support does not mean uncritical support. If you do something right, you should be praised. If you do something wrong, you should be held to account for what you have done and, in some cases, it will be appropriate for disciplinary action to be taken. No one gets things right all the time. What matters is the way in which the manager reacts to things that go wrong.

If something serious goes wrong, managers may react in very different ways. The first type of manager is one whose only interest, when a serious incident occurs, is to make sure that no blame is

45:   Greenleaf, R. K. 'Ages 20–40: What I did with those years', Box 1 Franklin Trask Library quoted in Frick. Op. cit.

attached to them. If they were not on duty when things went wrong, they are very quick to make sure that everyone knows that they were not there. They may well be eager to blame the staff who were there and to give the impression, or even say explicitly, that things would not have gone wrong had they been around. They make no attempt to identify themselves with their staff who were around and no attempt to encourage or support those who are in the firing line. In this situation people will not feel supported; they will feel abandoned and hung out to dry.

The second type of manager behaves very differently. If they were not around, it is important that they make it clear that they were not there when things went wrong. However, while they cannot take individual responsibility for what happened, they make it clear that, as the manager, they accept the appropriate degree of responsibility for what went wrong because the mistake has been made by their team. They do all that they can, while supporting a full investigation and appropriate disciplinary action, to encourage and support the staff and to help them to learn the lessons from what has occurred.

Staff will feel very differently in these two situations. In the second situation, they are much more likely to learn the lessons and to be open about future errors. The staff will feel that the manager is on their side. A head teacher, responsible for remarkable improvement in a "failing" school, was asked what the secret of his success was. He said that the staff felt that he was on their side. Where else should a head teacher be?

What happened

I was fortunate. Only once in my career did I have to work for someone who was not on my side. It was a debilitating experience and caused me considerable stress.

What I learned

It is very difficult to work for someone who does not want you to work for them, who would have preferred someone else, and who is not on your side. People need to feel supported. If you are a manager, you should support your staff, and they should feel your support, particularly when things go wrong and times are hard.

The second thing that people need from their manager is **feedback**, including appraisal. It is very important to receive feedback on your performance in a job, on how well you are doing your work. If we are not told how we are doing, how can we improve? The problem is that appraisal is a demanding process that requires many of the values and behaviours discussed in this chapter. The manager must take it seriously. They need to prepare so that they have reflected carefully on what to say and they need the evidence to support their conclusions so that you can understand exactly what has gone wrong and do something about it, or what has gone right so that you can build on what you have done. The manager also needs the courage to give you bad news, to be honest. This requires sensitivity, because even though it is important to know the truth, it is important to share the truth in a constructive way so that you can feel positive about changing the things you need to change. This is not easy! For many people the experience of appraisal includes complicated and lengthy forms that are filled in reluctantly and with difficulty followed by brief and less than honest discussions that leave you no wiser about what you are good at and what you are not good at. If appraisal is done properly, you should leave the discussion feeling valued for what you do well and very clear about what you need to do better. In my thirty-six years of full-time work I had only five good appraisals. These were carried out by the two best chairs I worked for as a chief executive, Rennie Fritchie in Gloucester and John Marshall in County Durham and Darlington. None of the appraisals carried out by managers met my needs.

What happened.

When I was a young manager at operational level, I did not understand the importance of good relationships with senior medical staff. They seemed to get along very nicely without me! Other people seemed to need my help more and made me feel more useful. This was, of course, a serious error of judgement. Nobody raised this issue with me until I discovered that the consultants were not happy with me and that I could not stay in my job. I was offered a more senior but non-operational job. However, to be moved against my will to a "staff" role was a major setback for me. I went home and cried all night. I woke up the next morning both angry and determined. I told my boss that I would leave but did not want the job he had offered me. I would find my own job. And I did!

What I learned

If I had been told about the issue earlier, I would have done something about it. As soon as I was told, I realised how foolish I had been. Consultant medical staff are very important people with great political power. They expect to be the centre of everyone's world, and they realised that they were not the centre of mine. When I got to my new job, I set out to build good relationships with the consultants, and I succeeded. I learned my lesson. If I had been given the opportunity to improve, I would have taken it, but it was too late for my previous role; the consultants had lost confidence in me.

The third thing that people need is development and **training**. As discussed in Chapter Two, developing people to their maximum capacity is at the heart of effective management. As J. K. Rowling reminds us, "It matters not what a man is born but what he grows to be."[46] Anyone who hopes to be a successful manager must take delight in the development of others. To see people grow, to see them become better at what they do, to see them achieve their potential, is one of the greatest satisfactions of management. When I retired from full-time work, I was able to count twelve people I had worked with who were or had been chief executives. I have seen people develop and grow.

It is important for managers to understand that the development of the people working with them is one of their most important

---

46:     Rowling, J. K. *Harry Potter and the Goblet of Fire* (2000)

responsibilities. They must make sure that resources for development and training are fairly distributed amongst the staff. The worst sort of manager is the manager who is only concerned about their own development and makes sure that everything they want to take part in is arranged and funded. A manager who does this sends a profound signal to their colleagues. They are saying clearly, given that actions speak louder than words, that they – the manager – are more important and significant than their colleagues, that their own development and training needs matter more. David Stoter was a hospital chaplain whom I had the privilege of working with, and he understood this very well. David helped me to understand that "training is a valuing exercise as well as an educative one".

The distribution of resources is important but it is less important than the values the manager brings to these decisions. Even if resources are very limited, a manager can take delight in the development of others. Thoughtlessness and selfishness play a part in the decisions of those managers who keep the resources to themselves. However, jealousy is also a significant factor. Some managers cannot bear the thought that their colleagues might grow to be better than they are, that they might be outshone by a junior colleague. Thy devote themselves to ensuring that those around them do not grow. Their concern is not to have the most effective team but to have a team that does not challenge them.

The best managers hope that their colleagues will grow to their full potential even if they grow to be more effective and highly regarded than the manager is. They know that what matters is that the job is done to the highest possible standard and that to achieve this every member of the team must be developed to their full capacity. The grace to take delight in the development of others is fundamental to effective management.

The fourth thing that people need from their manager is **clear job content**. As discussed in Chapter Four, simplicity is not a matter of shame and complexity is not an indication of brilliance. In my experience people crave clarity and simplicity. They want to know what is expected of them. People work most effectively when what is required of them is clear, and changes are properly explained to them. Consistency is very important. It is difficult when people are used to doing something one way – the accepted way – only to be told that they have been doing it the wrong way all along or that expectations have changed, and so must they. Managers who frequently change their expectations of their colleagues, and in particular those who do not explain changes, are very difficult to work with.

What happened

I worked for a brilliant and experienced man who made a huge contribution to the NHS. However, he was not an easy man. My job had a very wide remit, including planning and personnel. One of my first tasks was to prepare the district plan. I worked very hard, with the help of my excellent colleagues, and prepared the best draft I could possibly prepare. When it was finished, one of my colleagues and I met my boss to discuss the draft. He said nothing. After an awkward few minutes during which I waited patiently for him to speak, I asked my colleague to leave us so that I could find out what was going on. I thought he would speak more freely if there were only the two of us present. Eventually he said that I had left him nothing to do. He had clearly been hoping for a plan that would need considerable input from him. We talked it through and I think he came to see that my only desire was to do the best possible job and that I respected him and was very happy to learn from him.

What I learned

Make your expectations clear. If you want a draft that needs further work, say so. Don't regard good work as a challenge. Take delight in what your colleagues have done for you.

Now it's time to consider two more of our 40 questions.
18. Do you receive support, feedback (including appraisal and development) and training from your manager? Is your job content clear?

19. Do you provide support, feedback (including appraisal and development) and training to those you manage? Do you make sure they have clear job content?

As I explained at the beginning, Robert Greenleaf's thinking about leadership and management as the modern version of servant leadership has had a great impact on me. Greenleaf worked for AT&T from 1929 to 1964. His final role was as director of worldwide management research. He was regarded as the conscience of the company and as their Abe Lincoln. When he retired in 1964, he wanted to have a useful old age because "life is growth and when growth stops there is atrophy."[47] For twenty-six years, he taught and wrote about servant leadership. His first publication was *The Servant As Leader*.

Greenleaf has been hugely influential. Peter Senge tells "people not to waste their time reading all the other managerial leadership books... If you are really serious about the deeper territory of true leadership, read Greenleaf." Senge describes *The Servant As Leader* as the "most singular and important statement on leadership I have read in the last twenty years."[48]

Kenneth Blanchard, the author of *One Minute Manager* which sold more than 10 million copies, was enthralled with Greenleaf's thinking.[49]

Stephen Covey says that "the servant leadership concept is a principle, a natural law; getting our social value systems and personal habits aligned with this enobling principle is one of the greatest challenges of our lives."[50]

Warren Bennis says that "servant leadership is a counterbalance to the glorification, deification and lionisation of leaders who have neglected or forgotten what they are there for" and that "Robert Greenleaf's writings are among the most original, useful, accessible and novel on the topic of leadership."[51]

47: Greenleaf, R. K. 'Journal, 30 August 1940'. Franklin Trask Library Box 1, quoted in Frick. Op. cit.

48: Senge, Peter, in Spears, Larry (Ed). *Reflections on Leadership* (1995)

49: Blanchard, Kenneth and Peale, Vincent Norman. *The Power of Ethical Management* (1988)

50: Covey, Stephen. *Insights on Leadership: Service, Stewardship and Servant Leadership* (1998)

51: Bennis, Warren. Interview with Larry C. Spears, (2003), quoted in Frick. Op. cit.

The Ten Characteristics of the Servant Leader

Larry Spears, who was the president and chief officer of the Greenleaf Center for Servant Leadership from 1990–2007, defined the ten characteristics of the servant leader.[52]

Listening. Greenleaf said that listening is the premier skill and that leadership requires being a good listener. Greenleaf ran listening courses at Harvard. There were no listening courses at Cambridge. Most people at Cambridge wanted to talk; few wanted to listen. I have worked hard to learn to listen and hope that I am a much better listener than I once was. Listening starts with respect, with being alive to the strong possibility that someone else knows more than you do. I will discuss listening again when I consider Warren Bennis' ten hard questions for would-be leaders and managers in Chapter Six. John O'Brian made a powerful point about listening when he was discussing user empowerment: "When people not used to speaking out are heard by people not used to listening, then real change happens."[53]

Empathy – putting yourself in other people's shoes – is vital. Greenleaf knew many of the researchers involved in the famous Hawthorne project which is regarded as the turning point in the establishment of human relations thinking about management. Don M. Frick quotes Walter V. Bingham: "The ability and willingness of the supervisor to listen rather than to shout orders; to know and understand each worker in his group; to be genuinely interested but not domineering; these are some of the aspects of good supervision that turned out to be vastly more important than hours or rest periods or methods of payment in improving the mental attitudes of the employees and thereby increasing their productivity as well as their satisfaction."[54]

Empathy comes more naturally to some personality types than to others. However, everyone can develop empathy simply by consciously putting themselves in the shoes of the person they are dealing with. These empathy questions only take a few seconds but can be invaluable.

52:     Spears, Larry. *Reflections on Leadership* (1995)

53:     O'Brien, John. cadenceconsultants.co.uk

54:     Bingham, V. Walter. Management's Concern with Personnel in Industrial Psychology. *Harvard Business Review* (October 1931)

If you are going to ask someone to do something for you, take a moment to think about what it will mean for them. How difficult will it be? How much time will it take? Will it mean that they have to work longer hours, and will that have an impact on any caring responsibilities they may have or on other aspects of their personal life? These questions may lead you to realise that they are not the right person to ask or that it is not the right time to ask. Even if you have to ask, you will ask differently and they will hear your request differently if you have placed yourself in their shoes.

It is particularly important for people in senior positions to develop empathy. As Margaret Neale has pointed out: "Having power typically reduces a person's ability to understand how others think, see and feel."[55]

Healing applies both to individuals and to organisations. Individuals can be damaged by the way they have been treated by bosses, colleagues or by circumstances. The damage done can last for years as trust is lost and self-esteem is undermined. All of us can help the healing process. There is no quick fix. Trust will only be restored by the individual feeling that they can trust once again. Self-esteem will only be re-established when the individual is valued and made to feel worthwhile. Organisations can also be damaged by poor management and leadership. Again, there is no quick fix. The only remedy is management and leadership based on sound principles.

What happened

In 1985 I was invited to speak at the annual conference of the medical missions in East Africa. Leadership and management had been chosen as the theme. The King's Fund generously paid my fare, and the chairman I worked for allowed me to have the time off work. I said that I would only go if I could have a few days in East Africa before the conference. This was not because I wanted a jolly but because I did not want to use any of the material I normally used for NHS colleagues. I wanted to listen and learn before deciding what I could say that would be helpful to these remarkable people who ran mission hospitals in

55:    Neale, Margaret. Quoted by O'Hara, Carolyn, in *Harvard Business Review* (June 2014)

Kenya, Tanzania and Uganda. I spent some wonderful time at Chogoria Hospital, in the Meru district in the foothills of Mount Kenya. For a week, I met staff and patients, including the remarkable women who ran remote community clinics providing a wide range of advice, treatment and care.

Having listened, I realised that I needed to talk about leadership and management in terms that meant something to the people I had the privilege of speaking to. At the conference, I talked about sick and healthy organisations. The people I was sharing my thoughts with knew far more than I did about health and sickness. I explained that organisations could be sick and healthy too. A healthy hospital was one in which patients were at the centre of everyone's attention, where colleagues supported each other, where communication was good, where the people doing the managing listened to the people being managed. A sick hospital was the opposite of all these things. They got it!

What I learned

Healing is a part of leadership and management. Organisations as well as individuals may need healing. If you are going to teach, to share ideas, listen first. Put yourself in the shoes of those you are talking with and it is much more likely that what you say will be helpful.

Awareness. It is important to scan your environment, to seek to understand the world you are living in. If you close your mind, eyes and ears to what is going on around you, it is much less likely that you will be able to manage and to lead. Complacency is dangerous. Curiosity is vital. The desire to understand what is happening and respond to changing circumstances is fundamental to growth and development.

Persuasion is a key feature of servant leadership and management and is discussed in Chapter Four. Of course, there are situations in which orders have to be given, including situations of life and death, both in healthcare and in combat, where it is vital that something is done immediately and without question. However, in the vast majority of situations it is better to persuade than to give orders. Persuasion is difficult and time consuming but it is always worthwhile.

As already noted, Greenleaf used the word "convincement", which is very powerful.[56] If you can persuade people to the point where they believe for themselves, it will be much more rewarding and successful to manage and to lead. Greenleaf said that "not much that is really important can be accomplished with coercive power. Headship, the holding of a titular position or possessing coercive power, is not at all synonymous with leadership," and again, "The trouble with coercive power is that it only strengthens resistance … it is not organic. Only persuasion and the consequent voluntary acceptance are organic."[57]

Conceptualisation is the process of gaining perspective, setting goals, evaluation and analysis. This is very important in helping yourself and colleagues to relate your and their work to the work of the organisation. It is helpful if people understand where they fit in and why what they do is important.

Foresight is essential. Greenleaf described the failure to foresee as an ethical failure. If you care about what you do, it is essential to think about how your work is going to change. What is going to happen to the environment in which you work? What new developments are there going to be in your work and the way in which it is done? What new practice or research is coming along that will open up new possibilities and a better way of doing things?

Stewardship is one of my favourite words. It means looking after things. The most important thing to look after is yourself and the people you work with. If you don't look after yourself, you will not be able to look after others and you will not be able to manage and to lead. Being careless with the people on whom you depend is foolish. People need to be nurtured and looked after. If people feel that you are genuinely concerned for their well-being, they will be much more likely to be committed to what they do and loyal to you. So look after people but first look after yourself.

56:    Greenleaf, R. K. *The Servant As Leader* (1970)

57:    Ibid.

What happened

As mentioned in Chapter Three, in 1991 I faced a formidable combination of work pressures and personal problems. The work challenges were focused on dealing with the Wessex Regional Systems Information Plan, which is described in more detail later in this chapter. The personal problems related to the fact that at forty-three I was beginning to understand myself and to face up to who I was. I went to see my GP, who was an excellent doctor and a good man. I explained that I was in trouble and needed some psychotherapy or counselling. He was, as always, sympathetic and concerned. He explained that NHS waiting lists were long and that I was unlikely to get help for many months. Although I spent my working life in the NHS, and strongly support its principles, I have never criticised people who use private health care because I have always known that I would use it if the NHS could not provide what I or my family needed. I asked him to refer me for private treatment and the next day I was sharing my issues with a psychotherapist. Over the next nineteen years I received a great deal of support. After I went to Durham, I had the great good fortune to be supported by an excellent counsellor who I worked with for more than ten years and through some of the most difficult times in my life. Without his astonishing empathy, understanding and wisdom I would not be writing this book.

What I learned

Look after yourself. Seeking help is not a sign of weakness but of strength. There is no shame in seeking help and support. I learned that it was important for me to acknowledge publicly the support I had received. On many occasions, people who had heard me talk about it told me how much it had meant to them to know that someone in a senior role was willing to reveal their vulnerability and need for help. They often said that they felt I had made it possible for them to seek help.

Commitment to the growth of people. This was discussed earlier in this chapter and needs no further elaboration here. Just do it! Take delight in the development of others. You will grow too.

Building community. We all know what community feels like when it works well: the sense of belonging, of support, of acceptance, of appropriate interest and concern for our welfare. It is important that this exists in the workplace as well as in the places in which we live.

Here are questions 20–29 from our 40 questions for those aspiring to be servant leaders and managers.

20. Do you listen as well as talk?
21. Do you put yourself in other people's shoes, even if you have to make an effort because empathy does not come naturally to you?
22. Do you heal people and organisations?
23. Are you aware of the world around you?
24. Do you persuade people to the point of convincement?
25. Do you use your intellect to evaluate and analyse issues, to relate your work and the work of your colleagues to the work of the organisation as a whole?
26. Do you look ahead to see how your environment and the work you do is going to change?
27. Do you look after yourself and other people?
28. Do you take delight in the development of others?
29. Do you build community at work as well as at home?

As you answer these questions it would be good to keep in mind two wonderful thoughts: Greenleaf said, "The best test of servant leadership is, do those we serve grow as people?"[58]

Don Frick summarised Greenleaf's thoughts powerfully when he said, "The core idea of servant leadership is quite simple – authentic, ethical leaders those whom we trust and who we want to follow – are servants first... For Greenleaf an authentic leader is one who chooses to serve, and serve first, and then chooses to lead."[59]

58: Greenleaf, R. K. *Servant Leadership* (1977)

59: Frick, Don M. Op. cit.

Fifteen Essential Values and Behaviours

From my experience, from the things I have got wrong and the things I have got right, I believe managers need to think carefully about fifteen values and behaviours. It may seem a lot, but management and leadership are serious things. The first five values and behaviours are discussed here, and then we will move on to the Ten R's.

Passion for the work of the organisation. It is very difficult to manage or lead if you do not care about the work you are doing. Harvard's John Kotter, in his excellent research on successful chief executives in the private sector, concluded that the one characteristic that united them was their commitment to the work of their organisations.[60] In health care, where I have spent the great majority of my working life, it is vital that managers care about patients, service users and about the quality of the care and treatment they receive. If clinical staff, doctors and nurses, and many others, feel that a manager really cares about patients, it will transform their relationship with the manager. There will still be many difficult issues and many disagreements. However, the clinicians and the manager will be united by a shared goal – to provide outstanding patient treatment and care.

Empathy for the people your organisation serves – the customers – and for the people who serve – the frontline staff. Empathy has already been discussed in the consideration of the characteristics of the servant leader. Empathy is putting yourself in other people's shoes. It is because I believe that empathy is so important that I have chosen *Other People's Shoes* as the title for this book.

Humility. Nothing is more dangerous than arrogance. Some of the worst cases of neglect and mistreatment of patients have occurred because the person responsible for their care thought that they knew it all and had nothing to learn. It is important to have a proper sense of your own skills and abilities. Self-esteem is essential to confidence. However, a wise person will always be open to the possibility that they might be wrong, that someone else knows a better way, that even if they have been doing something for a long time, they will not necessarily

---

60:    Kotter, John. *The General Managers* (1982)

remain an expert or even competent. Humility enables us to learn from feedback and to be constantly aware of the vulnerability of our humanity.

Curiosity is the desire to learn, the desire to understand, the desire to do better. The importance of curiosity has also already been discussed in Chapter One. The quotation from Don Berwick was given there. Don reminds us that it is important that a learning environment is established where it is safe to admit that you do not know, and that we need to willingly place ourselves in the vulnerable position of saying, "I do not know how to do this but I have a way to find out." If managers and leaders are not curious it is unlikely that they will find out about what to do and how to do it. Greenleaf believed that it is better for leaders to admit they do not see the path more clearly than anyone else, that they ask for help from those they are leading and that they acknowledge that there will be times when someone else sees the path more clearly. Oliver Goldsmith understood the importance of learning from others: "People seldom improve if they have no other model but themselves to copy after."[61]

Rennie Fritchie introduced me to "Is this where I was going?" by Natasha Josefowitz. The poem powerfully conveys the truth that we are all potential learners and teachers and that this dual role makes us truly who we are.[62] **Integrity** is the quality of being honest and having strong moral principles. Integrity makes trust possible, and Greenleaf believed that trust is first and that nothing will move until trust is firm. We will think about trust again in Chapter Six when we go through Warren Bennis' hard questions for would-be leaders and managers. Trust takes a long time to establish and can be destroyed in an instant.

What happened

Towards the end of my career I had the privilege of managing and leading a major review of acute services. This was one of the most difficult

---

61: Goldsmith, Oliver. *The Bee No II* (1759)

62: Josefowitz, Natasha. *Is this where I was going?* (1983)

and rewarding experiences of my career and it taught me a lot about the value of integrity.

When I started the job, I knew part of the area well but I had not worked in the rest of the area for many years. The first thing I did was to meet the senior people from all the organisations I was going to be working with: NHS trusts, primary care groups and social services departments. I went to listen and to learn. I asked everyone the same question: what is the most important thing I can do in my new job? By the end of the process the answer was clear. The overwhelming view was that acute services would be very difficult to sustain in their existing form in two fairly small general hospitals. I was told that a number of reviews had been carried out that had not gone anywhere. The message to me was, *please do another one, and this time make it happen.* I accepted the challenge.

Working with the very able director of planning, Helen Bryne, and all my colleagues, we set about trying to do it properly. We involved the public, patients and carers. We involved frontline clinical staff. We were open with the media. We set up an expert clinical panel consisting of people with reputations as experts in their field. We worked closely with the local authority scrutiny committees and kept the MPs informed.

However, the work was always going to be controversial, because communities quite rightly value and defend their local services. This became clear when it became obvious that one of the hospitals would lose its emergency services. I felt that my job was under threat because I had fronted much of the community engagement and media work and I was very closely identified with the plans. It would have been very easy to compromise my integrity and withdraw the proposals. Indeed, the proposals were paused and externally reviewed. However, the review upheld our recommendations and they were subsequently implemented after being referred to the independent reconfiguration panel at national level. I believe that the people who live in the area have received safer and better care because of the work that we did in the review.

When the controversy was at its height I received two messages that are among the most encouraging feedback that I have ever received. I valued the words so greatly that I still carry copies of the messages in my encouragement and refreshment file that I keep in my back pack to consult when I need nourishment! I will give them in full because they mean so much to me.

> You will not remember me, Mr Jarrold, but I am indeed founder member of the Save our Hospital campaigners. On this particular occasion, I do not write to you on behalf of those lovely people. I am moved to simply contact you on my own behalf. You and I have disagreed on many things and we will continue to do so. However, I am much more comfortable dealing with a man of your integrity than with these "emerging campaigners" who came along (for political reasons). I am determined to say to you, here and now, that I always recognise the consistency of your considered opinions and I confirm that I much prefer them to the spin which is now being proffered by others. I would be pleased to meet with, and indeed to disagree with, you again!

> In my opinion throughout the review Ken Jarrold [this message was taken by my PA] has remained constant and true in what he has been saying. Although we disagree on the hospital issue, I have never doubted Mr Jarrold's honesty, integrity and professional approach. I watched Ken Jarrold on television last night and it is obvious what is going on. The political interference is obvious. I find it scandalous, distasteful and really wrong. The review is being used as a political pawn. I, and some of my campaign colleagues, are not blind to what is going on. It is destroying the credibility of the review. I know that Mr Jarrold is as straight as an arrow.

What I learned

Integrity works even in the most difficult situations. Integrity creates trust. Even people who disagree with you will respect and trust you if you have integrity. As Warren Bennis and James O'Toole remind us, "Real leaders demonstrate integrity, provide meaning, generate trust and communicate values."[63] I was also reassured by the words of Martin Luther King Jnr: "The ultimate test of a man is not where he stands in moments of comfort and convenience but where he stands at times of challenge and controversy."[64]

And now to the Ten R's!

1. **Realism.** We need to see the world as it is and not as we would wish it to be. Marcus Aurelius was clear about this in his Meditations, written in the second century AD: "Look things in the face and know them for what they are."[65]

    Realism is essential to strategic change. For me strategy is about three simple steps. First, decide where you want to be. You must describe clearly where you want to be. You need to show the way. Second, you must be realistic about where you are now. Third, you must plan the detailed steps that will take you from where you are now to where you want to be. If you are not realistic, your process of strategic change will fail. If you are too optimistic about where you are now, vital steps will be missed and issues left unresolved.

    It is so easy for people in senior roles to lose touch with reality. *The Emperor's New Clothes* is a very old and very helpful story. People could see that the emperor was delusional and did not want to hear the truth. As noted in Chapter Two, John Harvey Jones reminded us that chief executives should "value the people who bring you the bad news."[66] If you are in a senior role and you give the impression that you only want to hear the good news, then that is what you will get. You will drift along in blissful ignorance until it is too late to make changes. You will lose credibility and trust because people will see that you are deluding yourself. See the world as it is!

2. **Responsibility.** We need to take responsibility for our own actions and for the roles we are given. Some people feel that they cannot

63:     Bennis, Warren and O'Toole, James. Don't Hire the Wrong CEO. *Harvard Business Review* (May–June 2000)

64:     King, Martin Luther. *Strength to Love* (1963)

65:     Aurelius, Marcus. *Meditations* (161–180 AD)

66:     Harvey-Jones, John. *Making It Happen* (1988)

manage and aspire to lead in accordance with the behaviours and values set out in this book because they work in an organisation, or part of an organisation, where these values and behaviours are not respected and practised. It is, of course, much more difficult to do the right thing in such an environment. However, the nature of the organisation that we are working in does not absolve us from doing our best to manage and lead in accordance with the values in which we believe and the behaviours we attempt to practice. We are responsible for our own actions. Even in an unsympathetic organisation we can do our best to behave in accordance with our values. It is natural to replicate bad behaviour that we experience ourselves. If we are bullied, it is tempting to bully others. However, if we try to manage and lead in accordance with these values, we will not bully others just because we are bullied ourselves. Unless you are the chief executive, you are not responsible for the organisation as a whole. Unless you are head of the department or manager of the team you are not responsible for the department or the team. You are responsible for yourself. It is easy to blame others or to take the view that there is nothing we can do. The toughest self-discipline is to take responsibility for what we do and say.

3. **Respect**. We know when we are respected. Are we being allowed to talk? Are we being listened to? Do people look at us when they are speaking to us? Do they remember our names? Do they think about what we want and need? Respect is fundamental in all our relationships with managers, colleagues and those we manage and aspire to lead. Respect for customers is fundamental in every organisation. In health services respect for patients, service users and carers is the most important value and the most important behaviour.

4. **Responsiveness**. It is not enough just to listen and respect. We need to respond. If managers, colleagues or customers ask us to do something, it is vital to respond. Of course, we will not always be able to do what is asked of us, but we can always respond and explain why we have not been able to do what we were asked to do. The vast majority of people have reasonable expectations.

They understand resource and time constraints. They know that they cannot have everything they want. However, they appreciate being told what they can and can't have and why they can't have some things. One of the things that staff and customers find most difficult is not being told why things cannot be done. In staff and customer consultation it is as important to explain why things have not been done as it is to report back on what has been done.

5. **Resilience** and **resolve** are fundamental to management and leadership. Few worthwhile things are easy. Most of us experience frequent setbacks. Luck plays its part but often the most successful people – the most effective leaders and managers – are not necessarily the most able; rather they are often the most persistent. They do not give up when things do not go well. They try again and go on trying until it becomes clear that they cannot succeed or the cost of trying outweighs the benefits of achieving the objective. Benjamin Disraeli reminded us that "the secret of success is constancy of purpose."[67]

6. **Reflection**. Arrogance does not lead to reflection. Arrogant people think that there is no need to reflect. What good would that be when they are already perfect? They think they know best and have no interest in wondering if they could have done better. Arrogance is profoundly dangerous and is a frequent factor when things go badly wrong. Humility is a precondition for reflection. If you are open to the possibility that you could do better, learn more, that you may not always know best, then you will want to reflect. I try to reflect every day and ask myself some very simple questions:
   - What have you done well today?
   - What could you have done better?
   - Have I behaved in accordance with my values?
   - Do I need to apologise to anyone for the way in which I have behaved?

If there is a need to apologise, I try and do it as soon as possible. No one expects us to behave well all the time. People understand that even if we usually behave well, our behaviour will sometimes

---

67:    Disraeli, Benjamin. *Endymion* (1880)

be affected by stress. Apologies will usually be accepted if openly and sincerely given with an explanation if that is appropriate.

7. **Reliability** is a basis for trust, and as already noted, Robert Greenleaf believed that trust is first and that nothing will move until trust is firm. If you are reliable, people are more likely to trust you. Reliability is about doing what you will say you will do, explaining why you cannot do what you said you would do, and being consistent. It is very difficult for your colleagues if your behaviour is not reasonably consistent. They need to know how you do things and how you want other people to do things. If you manage people, it is very important to make your expectations clear and to explain if your expectations change. It is very difficult for staff if they are praised for doing something one day and criticised for doing it the same way the next day. If you are operating a shift system with shift managers it is important that they agree how things should be done so that if staff are working a shift they do not normally work, or with a shift manager they do not normally work with, they still have a good understanding of what is expected of them and of how things should be done.

8. **Recognition**. It is very important to recognise the achievements of others and never to take credit for other people's achievements. The opportunity to say well done should be taken whenever possible. Even the most cynical and hardened of colleagues will appreciate recognition. It is good practice for organisation to arrange events where staff are recognised for their work. Properly done, the events can mean a great deal to those whose achievements are recognised and be good for the morale of the staff as a whole. However, it is the day-to-day simple praise and thanks that matter even more. Indeed, the beneficial effect of award events will be completely undermined if staff work every day in an environment where praise and thanks are rarely given. If people are publicly recognised for their work, it is important that the selection process for awards is conducted fairly and carefully. It is vital to avoid favouritism or cronyism of any kind. The key test is whether, when colleagues are praised, other staff feel that the praise is deserved. Recognition systems can be easily

undermined if it is clear that staff are being praised because they get on with the people responsible for the selection process rather than because their work is of value to the organisation. Fairness is key.

It is also important to be able to do the right thing without any guarantee of recognition. The famous quotation attributed to Harry Truman, based on Benjamin Jowett, makes this point: "It is amazing what you can accomplish when you do not care who gets the credit."[68]

What happened

As previously mentioned, one of the most difficult things I have ever dealt with was sorting out the Regional Information Systems Plan (RISP) in the Wessex Region. I was at home one weekend in the summer of 1989 when the chairman of the Wessex Regional Health Authority phoned to ask if I would be interested in applying for the post of regional general manager, the chief executive role in today's terms. I was, of course pleased and flattered. I had been a district general manager for more than seven years and I was ready for a change. I applied and was very fortunate to be appointed.

Although I had four wonderful years in Wessex, working with some very able people and achieving a great deal with them, much of my time and energy was spent on sorting out RISP. It soon became clear that I was dealing with the biggest IT failure the NHS had experienced. We estimated that £40 million had been wasted. This was nothing compared to the money wasted by the NHS Programme for IT/ Connecting for Health Programme (NPFIT) between 2005 and 2013.[69] However, it was a lot of money in the early 1990s.

The full story of RISP deserves a book by itself. However, it is sufficient here to note that there were two major problems. First, despite the excellent vision for IT, the system was not supported by many in Wessex, including influential doctors. Secondly, the contracts

---

68: Truman, Harry. Based on Jowett, Benjamin, *the Oxford Book of Aphorisms*

69: King, Anthony and Crewe, Ivor. *The Blunders of Our Governments* (2013)

negotiated with the private sector were not value for money and did not protect the interests of the NHS. I realised early on that the system could not be made to work and that the issue was one that would attract the attention of the Public Accounts Committee of the House of Commons. I also knew that there would be little credit for sorting it out and every opportunity for blame.

Fortunately, my sense of duty was strong enough to see me through with the help of my colleagues and some excellent legal advice. I found the courage to tell the chief executive of the NHS, and the Wessex chairman, that RISP could not be made to work. Then I summoned the resilience to get the best possible deal from the private sector contractors, and, with the expert help of Ian Dillow and his excellent public relations team, the opportunity to tell the story openly and clearly. The Public Accounts Committee hearing lasted for four hours. It was extremely difficult. There was no recognition for the work I had done. There was criticism for the decision I had made to pay off a senior colleague. I realised that I was the sacrificial lamb offered for the entertainment of the members of the committee. After the committee hearing I got on a train and was violently sick. The reason for my sickness was the release of tension after two and a half years of dealing with a very challenging issue.

What I learned

The lack of recognition was hurtful at the time. However, it is important to do the right thing without any guarantee of recognition. Doing the right thing is enough in itself.

9. **Risk**. Managers and those aspiring to leadership need to be willing to take risks. Carefully considered risk is an essential element of progress. If success has to be assured before decisions are taken only the safest and least adventurous decisions will ever be made. One of the issues that helped me to understand this is the recovery of people with mental illness. As they recover, people need to be able to take risks. If a risk-free care pathway was adopted, there would be little chance of recovery.

10. **Reason** and **rationality**. We need to base our decisions on values and evidence as well as on self-interest and opinion. We need to explain our decisions, to persuade and to convince. I have seen many decisions taken on the basis of self-interest and opinions. As I explained in Chapter One, I learned early on that when staff objected to changes on the grounds that the changes would adversely affect patients, it was sometimes the case that the only adverse effect would be on them. They realised that harm to patients was a more convincing reason for resisting change than their desire to avoid inconvenience to themselves. Also, early on I was amazed at how people with a very high level of scientific education, who had been trained to demand the highest quality of evidence in their work, would regard evidence as totally irrelevant on topics which mattered greatly to them but were outside their professional expertise; for instance, car parking! In consultations about difficult service changes communities rightly defend their self-interest and arguments based on opinions are often more attractive than the facts. Whenever we are confronted with self-interest and opinion, we need to hang on to our values and look hard for the evidence. Above all we need to exercise judgement – the ability to make considered decisions or come to sensible conclusions. As Clement Attlee reminded us: "A lot of clever people have everything except judgement."[70] J. K. Rowling made a similar and a powerful point: "It is our choices that show what we truly are, far more than our abilities."[71]

A fifteen-part question for reflection and learning

30. Reflect on the extent to which you are able to manage and lead in accordance with the five values and assess yourself against the Ten R's set out here:
    - Passion

70: Attlee, Clement. Quoted in Williams, Francis, *Twilight of Empire: Memoirs of Prime Minister Clement Attlee* (1962)

71: Rowling, J. K. *Harry Potter and the Chamber of Secrets* (1998)

- Empathy
- Humility
- Curiosity
- Integrity
- Realism
- Responsibility
- Respect
- Responsiveness
- Resilience
- Reflection
- Reliability
- Recognition
- Risk
- Reason and rationality

Chapter Six

Hard Questions for Leaders and Managers

One of the most helpful things I have come across is the list of hard questions for managers and leaders prepared by Warren Bennis and James O'Toole.[72] They really are hard questions! The questions are so challenging that I recommend that they are not asked too frequently. Despite many years of experience, learning and reflection I am never able to answer them all positively. These hard questions are a great way of keeping on track. Just don't depress yourself by asking them too often! Have compassion for yourself. Bennis and O'Toole provide questions 31 to 39.

31.   Do you lead consistently in a way that inspires followers to trust you?

I broaden the question to ask myself if I behave in a way that inspires people to trust me – bosses, staff, leaders, followers and colleagues. As previously noted, Robert Greenleaf believed that trust is first, nothing will move until trust is firm. Trust takes a very long time to establish and is very easy to destroy. In our personal lives, we can be in a trusting relationship for many years and then one day one partner does something which destroys trust and it may be impossible to rebuild. The same is true at work. We can have a close and trusting working relationship with

---

72:   Bennis, Warren and O'Toole, James. 'Don't Hire the Wrong CEO'. *Harvard Business Review* (May–June 2000)

someone for many years and then we find out that they have blamed us for something we did not do, taken credit for something we did do, or bad-mouthed us to managers and colleagues. The trust built up over the years will be destroyed in an instant. This is immensely challenging because trust is based on what we do and not on what we say. Do we believe that someone loves us because they say they love us or because they behave in a way that demonstrates their love for us? It is easy to say that you love someone. It is very difficult to live a loving life. Our managers, staff and colleagues will not trust us because of what we say. They will trust us because of what we do. As someone who has come to gardening late in life I see a powerful illustration of this in looking after plants. It may take years to bring a plant to maturity. It only takes one hard frost, or a failure to water during a dry spell, to destroy it.

32. Do you hold people accountable for their performance and promises?

Organisations do not exist to provide jobs although that may be a very helpful by-product. Organisations exist to serve customers. When someone signs a contract to work for an organisation they make promises about their conduct, including the hours to be worked and the tasks to be performed. If a member of staff is not fulfilling their promises, is not delivering good performance, then action must be taken. If it is not taken, customers will receive a poor service and/or colleagues may have to cover for the person who is not performing. I learned this lesson very early on in my career. In Chapter Three I told the stories of the surgical barber who drank, the porters who regularly took one-day sick leave and the senior colleague who was lazy. If managers fail to deal with poor performance, the quality of service will suffer and staff will resent having to cover for colleagues who are allowed to break their promises. The way in which managers respond should, of course, depend on the circumstances. If someone is trying hard but not delivering, it is important to do everything possible to support them in an attempt to improve performance. Training, education, coaching and mentoring may all help. If someone is not trying, then close supervision is required until either performance is improved or the person moves on voluntarily or as the result of disciplinary action. Holding people to account for their performance and promises requires many of the qualities previously discussed, including courage and resilience. It is also important for leaders and managers to keep their promises. Pollard reminds us, "Our word and the promises we make to each other provide the framework for relationships to grow. Leaders must keep their promises to the people they lead even if it is at their own personal risk and sacrifice. It is their obligation."[73]

33. Are you comfortable delegating important tasks to others?

It is very important that work is distributed fairly and that the difficult tasks are shared out in a fair way. One of the most dangerous things a manager can do is to avoid all the difficult work themselves and give it to the most junior or inexperienced staff or the ones least likely to say no. Staff really resent being given all the difficult stuff to do while the manager, and their favourites, get to do the fun stuff. Never behave in a way that causes staff or colleagues to say that their days consist of the things you do not want to do. The tough stuff should always be shared.

34. How much time do you spend developing other leaders?
35. How much time do you spend communicating your vision, purpose and values? Do people down the line apply your vision to their day-to-day work?

I have put these two questions together because they are very closely related. Busy managers and busy leaders might well take the view that they do not have time to develop other managers and leaders if that means running workshops or courses or providing intensive coaching or mentoring. They don't have to! The best way to develop other managers and leaders is to be the best manager or leader you can be so that someone many years from now tells the story of what they learned from you, or better still, manage and lead in the way you inspired them to do. As I explained in Chapter One, I learned a huge amount from Jack

73:    Pollard, C. William. The Leader Who Serves, in Hessebein, F., Goldsmith, M., and Beckard, R. The Leader of the Future. Jossey Bass (1996)

Newton. Jack never gave me a seminar on management and leadership. He never wrote a paper for me to read. He just did his job in the best way he could, and I learned the lessons I continue to live by today.

The same is true about communicating vision, purpose and values. People are more likely to apply these things if they have seen you do them. Don't tell your new colleagues that you believe in integrity, humility and treating people well. They will think you are barmy! Just do it! Act with integrity, be humble and treat people well. If they see you doing these things and see the good effect it has on morale and performance, they will apply the values they have seen in action to their own work.

36. How comfortable are you sharing information, resources, praise and credit?

Never take the credit for another person's work. I was delivering a workshop on management and leadership in an NHS trust and when I reached this question a member of the group asked if he could tell his story. He had prepared a presentation, which had been very well received in the trust. His manager had then delivered the same presentation to a group at the next level up, the Strategic Health Authority. The work had once again been very well received. However, the manager claimed the work as their own and did not mention the person who had prepared it. The member of our group was understandably distressed and resentful at this behaviour. Even though the incident had occurred some time before he told us the story, his feelings were still raw. It is unlikely that this incident would be forgotten or forgiven. If the chief executive of your organisation visits your team to praise your work, make sure that the people directly responsible for the work being praised are introduced to the chief executive and receive the praise or are told about it afterwards if they are not available. If they hear that you have accepted the praise without referring to them, they will not forgive you easily. If they know that you made it clear where the credit lay, they will respect you for your honesty and values.

37. Do you energise others?

It is important to energise others particularly if you are in a management role or aspiring to lead. Of course it is wise to share your personal problems with colleagues so that they know what you are going through. Of course managers and leaders are human beings who need support and encouragement. However, in the workplace, in relating to the team you manage or the people you seek to lead, it is important not to drag people down! In my last chief executive role, I worked with a wonderful colleague who was our director of nursing. There were times in the management team meetings when I lacked energy because of the personal and work stress that I was experiencing. On one occasion my colleague had a word with me in the break. They said that they all understood what I was going through because I had shared much of it with them. However, a lack of energy was affecting them and making difficult to make progress in our discussions. My colleague was absolutely right. I needed support, but I got that from my wonderful counsellor. In the workplace I needed to energise those I managed and sought to lead. If you are going through a difficult break-up or divorce it is wise to tell your colleagues so that they understand why you are referring to your former partner in such unflattering terms! However, don't go on about it all day. You will drag them down.

38.   Do you consistently demonstrate respect for others?

We know when we are being respected. Does the person we are interacting with look at us? Do they listen to us? Do they remember our name, who we are and what we do? Do they appear to be genuinely interested in what we are doing and saying? Do they demonstrate consideration for us in their actions? Respect is fundamental to trust and to good relationships. To be respected is a very powerful motivator and develops our self-worth and self-respect. To be disrespected can destroy confidence and proper self-esteem. J. K. Rowling understands this well: "If you want to know what a man is like, take a good look at how he treats his inferiors, not his equals."[74]

74:   Rowling, J. K. *Harry Potter and the Goblet of Fire* (2000)

39.   Do you really listen?

As I said in Chapter Five, Greenleaf said that listening is the premier skill and he ran listening courses at Harvard. Listening starts with respect, with being alive to the strong possibility that someone else knows more than you do.

I often illustrate this point by talking about a patient going to see their GP. They tell the GP that they have not been sleeping well, they have lost their appetite and their bowels are not working normally. A GP who has not learned to listen will turn to the computer, as research shows many doctors do for a third of the time they are with patients. The doctor will prescribe something to help the patient sleep, something to stimulate appetite and something to get the bowels moving again. This is not helpful. A doctor who has learned to really listen will look at the patient and ask if something has happened in their life recently. The patient may say that their partner died some weeks ago but that is not too much of a problem because the relationship was not good. However, their cat died last week and that was a real tragedy because the cat was much loved! The doctor may then refer the patient for bereavement counselling, explaining that the referral has to be for the partner but will encourage the patient to talk about the death of the cat. The doctor may also suggest getting a new cat when the grieving process allows. That doctor has really listened.

The Native Americans have a wonderful phrase about listening. They refer to listening to where the words come from. The doctor who really listened found out where the words came from. If a colleague shares something with you, think about where the words come from. If you are busy at the time, go back the next day and ask about what was said. In the health care situation, your colleague may have expressed general concern about a patient but not felt able to be specific. Go back and ask what lay behind the concern. Your colleague may then feel able to tell you more. If you really listen, if you ask where the words come from, you are far more likely to be able to do the right thing.

Greenleaf also said:

- "The natural servant's response to any problem is to listen first."[75]
- "True listening builds strength in other people."[76]
- "In saying what I have on my mind, will I really improve on the silence?"[77]
- Listening is the premier skill.

What happened

As I have explained more than once(!), I have been very stressed at times as a result of a combination of work and personal pressures. At one stage I became convinced that I had a significant physical illness. I went to my doctor. I am very fortunate to have a wonderful doctor who, together with my counsellor, has seen me through many very difficult times. I first met him when I was sharing my thoughts on leadership and management with a group of GPs who were on a leadership development programme. I was impressed by him and asked, through an intermediary, if he would take me on, even though I did not live in his practice area. He agreed and I have been very fortunate to be a patient at an excellent practice, which is part of the social wealth of an area of Stockton on Tees that has many challenges. I am deeply grateful for his expertise, intelligence, compassion and patience. On this occasion he really listened, as usual, and referred me for tests. I don't know if he thought there might be a genuine physical problem or whether he realised that I was very stressed and not yet ready to face up to the work and personal problems. In the end after a number of tests, which showed no abnormalities, the very experienced gastroenterologist looked at me over his glasses and informed me that there was nothing physically wrong with me and asked me if I had that considered it might be stress. By then I was ready to hear this advice and soon after decided to take early retirement. The symptoms disappeared.

75:   Greenleaf, R. K. *The Servant As Leader* (1970)

76:   Ibid.

77:   Ibid.

What I learned

I learned that real listening can transform lives. I also learned that our physical and mental health is very closely connected and that stress can cause real and imagined physical symptoms. I learned that I was not strong enough to deal with the combination of personal and work pressures that I was facing and that something needed to change. Leaving full-time work removed the work stress. There followed two years of extreme personal stress much of which was self-inflicted. I survived because I had excellent support and because only one aspect of my life was in crisis. It has been my experience that the most difficult times are those when you are facing both personal and work stress. In this situation, there seems to be no refuge, nowhere to lay your burdens down, no safe place to grieve and begin to recover and rediscover joy.

Conclusion

I hope these thoughts and stories have been helpful. My only desire is to share what I have learned in the hope that it will be useful to others who are learning to manage and to lead.

This book is about trying to understand what leadership and management are, about why they are important, about human nature and about the values and behaviours required in leadership and management.

As managers and leaders, we must always remember that the most important people in any organisation are the customers – in a hospital, the patients and the carers – and the next most important people are the frontline staff. The rest of us – the managers and leaders – are there to serve the staff who serve the customers. We should never have something that is better than can be provided for the patients and staff. We are servants first.

Leadership and management are very different things. It is very unhelpful that many people, in their writing and speaking, do not define leadership and management but instead use the terms interchangeably. If we are to have any chance of learning to lead and manage, we must understand exactly what we are trying to do.

- Leadership is showing the way – showing what to do next. Leadership is not dependent on role or seniority. Leadership can come from anyone who can show the way.
- Management is the responsibility for the use of resources. Management is dependent on role and seniority.

Understanding what leadership and management are is the first step in developing as a leader and a manager. Once this is understood, it is possible to move on to think about the values and behaviours needed for leadership and management.

Of course, knowledge of your work, professional and technical expertise, and experience are all important in building credibility in leadership and management. However, values and behaviour are vital. What we do, and what we say, what we believe and who we are, make a huge impact on our effectiveness as leaders and managers and on those we manage and aspire to lead. This is often ignored or underplayed in discussions on leadership and management. This may be because it is very challenging to realise that every single thing we do and say, what we believe and who we are, impacts on our credibility and on others. It is so much easier to rely on qualifications, knowledge or experience. But qualifications, knowledge and experience will only take us so far. If we want to grow as leaders and managers, if we want to serve, we have to be willing to reflect on our behaviour and to learn the values and behaviours that will enable us to flourish.

For much of my time as a manager, and as someone aspiring to leadership, I had to believe that leadership and management were important. For many years, it was an article of faith. I learned from experience that you will only achieve real change, you will only improve performance, if you get the best from the people on whom your success depends. I also learned that you get the best from people through leadership and management.

However, it was not until much later in my career that the research-based evidence became available as a result of the work of Beverly Alimo-Metcalfe, Michael West and others. The research shows that leadership and management make a difference to the well-being of staff, to getting things done and to the quality of service provided for customers.

Leadership and management are about getting the best out of people. It makes sense, therefore, to think about human nature. As with everything else it is important to be realistic and to see human nature as it is and not as we would like it to be. The vast majority of people whom I have worked with and encountered in my personal life are genuine, hardworking and trustworthy. I have seen and experienced human nature at its best.

However, I have also seen human nature at close to its worst. I have seen carelessness, laziness, indifference, cruelty, jealously, untrustworthiness, dishonesty and selfishness.

If you aspire to lead and to manage it is important to be realistic about human nature. Certainly it is good to look for the best, but it is also wise to expect the worst!

As well as thinking about human nature in general terms, it is vital to understand ourselves and each other. When we understand ourselves, we can then try to be true to ourselves. We can appreciate our strengths, fulfil our needs and learn to compensate for our weaknesses. Know yourself and be true to yourself.

Robert Greenleaf's advocacy of servant leadership instantly appealed to me because it resonated with the values I acquired from my parents' deep Christian faith (they were missionaries) and which have remained with me in my journey to becoming a Christian agnostic. The concept of service was real to me from my earliest days. However, it was working for Jack Newton, at the Royal Hospital in Sheffield, that brought Greenleaf's thinking alive for me in the context of NHS management. I now had a theory – a way of thinking – and the practical example of Jack's service to the patients, relatives and frontline staff. I could see what a servant leader and manager could achieve. One of the most helpful things I have come across is the list of hard questions for managers and leaders prepared by Warren Bennis and James O'Toole.[78] They have been included in my own list of 40 Questions for reflection and learning.

When I retired from full-time work, someone asked me what values had guided me through my thirty-six years as a manager and someone who had aspired to lead. It was not a difficult question to answer. Four values have guided me and guide me still.

First, the most important people are the customers – in my world the patients, service users and carers. I have always tried to keep close to them and to have them in my mind and in my heart.

78:     Bennis, Warren, and O'Toole, James. Op. cit.

Don Berwick's words have lived with me: "To become the servant of the patient. To bring the patient into care. To use the patient's knowledge and experience. To shift from the patient as a guest in our service to us as the guest in the patient's life."[79]

Second, the next most important people are the frontline staff. If anyone needs to be reminded about who the most important staff are, they should just ask themselves what will cause greater disruption to service provision, a junior doctor in the Accident and Emergency Department who does not turn up to work or the chief executive who is absent?

Third, the managers, those who aspire to lead and the non-executive members of the board are there to serve the frontline staff. They are servants first.

Fourth, what matters is who you are, what you do, what you say and how you behave towards others.

These values bring us to the last question:

40. Do you put customers first and do you put frontline staff next?

Given the enormous influence that Robert Greenleaf has had on my thinking and on my work, it seems right to leave the last word to Don Frick's wonderful summary of Greenleaf's views: "The core idea of servant leadership is quite simple – authentic, ethical leaders, those whom we trust and who we want to follow, are servants first... for Greenleaf an authentic leader is one who chooses to serve, and serve first, and then chooses to lead."[80]

79:   Berwick, Don. Op. cit.

80:   Frick, Don M. Op. cit.

Questions for Reflection and Learning

As I noted earlier, Rennie Fritchie suggested when reading this book that it would be a good idea to answer these questions in dialogue with a colleague who you respect and trust. This seems to me a great idea. Reflection with a colleague can be very valuable.

1. What are your definitions of leadership and management, and do your definitions help you to grow as a leader and manager?

2. Can you think of people you have known who were leaders even though they were not managers?

3. Can you think of managers you have worked with who were also leaders?

4. Can you think of managers who were not leaders but encouraged leadership in others?

5. Can you think of managers who could not lead themselves but discouraged leadership from others because they felt threatened?

6. Reflecting on your own experience, which of these situations worked best in terms of the well-being of the team and the team's effectiveness in getting things done?

7. Do you have a realistic view of human nature?

8. Do you look for the best but also expect the worst?

9. When things go badly wrong do you display the worst of human nature by leaving your staff to their fate or do you show the best of human nature by supporting them and being on their side while fully cooperating in the investigation and any necessary disciplinary action?

10. When performance is poor, do you assess the causes carefully, providing support, training, coaching and supervised practice where the cause is a lack of experience or expertise, and dealing firmly and fairly with the individual if the cause is laziness or indifference?

11. Do you put customers and conscientious staff first by dealing with the staff who are not delivering?

12. Do you understand yourself?

13. Have you used Myers–Briggs or other approaches to help you to understand yourself and others?

14. Are you true to yourself?

15. Do the four behaviours described in Chapter Four make sense to you based on your experience of leading and being led?

    · courage to show the way
    · clearly and simply explaining what needs to be done
    · persuading people to follow
    · enabling others to lead when you do not know the way

16. Have you observed other behaviours that enhance or undermine leadership?

17. If you agree that the behaviours described in Chapter Four are desirable, how easy have you found it to demonstrate them when you have aspired to lead?

18. Do you receive support, feedback (including appraisal and development) and training from your manager? Is your job content clear?

19. Do you provide support, feedback (including appraisal and development) and training to those you manage? Do you make sure they have clear job content?

20. Do you listen as well as talk?

21. Do you put yourself in other people's shoes, even if you have to make an effort because empathy does not come naturally to you?

22. Do you heal people and organisations?

23. Are you aware of the world around you?

24. Do you persuade people to the point of convincement?

25. Do you use your intellect to evaluate and analyse, to relate your work and the work of your colleagues to the work of the organisation as a whole?

26. Do you look ahead to see how your environment and the work you do is going to change?

27. Do you look after yourself and other people?

28. Do you take delight in the development of others?

29. Do you build community at work as well as at home?

30. Reflect on the extent to which you are able to manage and lead in accordance with the five values set out in Chapter Five:

- Passion/commitment
- Empathy
- Humility
- Curiosity
- Integrity

And assess yourself against the Ten R's.

- Realism
- Responsibility
- Respect
- Responsiveness

- Resilience
- Reflection
- Reliability
- Recognition
- Risk
- Reason and rationality

31. Do you lead consistently in a way that inspires followers to trust you?

32. Do you hold people accountable for their performance and promises?

33. Are you comfortable delegating important tasks to others?

34. How much time do you spend developing other leaders?

35. How much time do you spend communicating your vision, purpose and values? Do people down the line apply your vision to their day-to-day work?

36. How comfortable are you sharing information, resources, praise and credit?

37. Do you energise others?

38. Do you consistently demonstrate respect for others?

39. Do you really listen?

40. Do you put customers first and do you put front line staff next?

Thoughts on Leadership and Management

In this final chapter I share some of the thoughts on leadership and management that have helped me on my journey of experience and learning. Managers and leaders do not always have the time to read widely and to find the useful stuff. I thought it would be helpful to collect some of them here for you.

The people who have influenced me most are:
- Robert Greenleaf
- Reg Revans
- John Kotter
- Warren Bennis
- Jim Collins
- Beverly Alimo-Metcalfe
- Michael West
- Don Berwick

"The best leader is hardly noticed. The next best is honoured and acclaimed. The worst is feared and despised. When the work of a good leader is done, the people say, 'We did this ourselves.' To lead the people, walk behind them."

—Lao Tzu, 600 BC

"Look things in the face and know them for what they are, remembering that it is your duty to be a good man. Do without flinching what man's nature demands; say what seems to you most just – though with courtesy, modesty and sincerity."

— Marcus Aurelius, AD 121–180

"Let not princes complain of the faults committed by the people subjected to their authority, for they result entirely from their own negligence or bad example."

— Discourses on Livy, *Niccolo Machiavelli, 1531*

"It must be considered that there is nothing more difficult to carry out, nor more dangerous to handle, than to initiate a new order of things. For the reformer has enemies in all those who profit by the old order and only lukewarm defenders in all those who would profit by the new order. This arises partly from the incredulity of mankind who do not believe in anything new until they have an actual experience of it."

— The Prince, *Niccolo Machiavelli, 1532*

"Nearly all men can stand adversity, but if you want to test a man's character, give him power."

— Abraham Lincoln

Hard-schooled by long power
Yet most humble of mind
Where ought that he was
Might advantage mankind.
Leal servant, loved master
Rare commander, sure guide.

"Great Heart", a poem about Theodore Roosevelt by Rudyard Kipling

"Managers are necessary; leaders are essential. Leadership is of the spirit, compounded by personality and vision. Management is of the mind, more a matter of accurate calculation, statistics, methods, timetables and routine."

— Field Marshal Sir William Slim

"Character is a question of values, inclinations and judgement, all of which are brought to bear in the day-to-day work of leadership."

—A Question of Character: A Life of John F. Kennedy,
Thomas C. Reeves

"Kennedy appeared, we clapped and cheered. He spoke to us for half an hour, and we were transfixed. He congratulated us on our scholarships; he told us that the president is no better than the people who elected him."

—*Andreas Hadjivassiliou, recalling a meeting*
addressed by President Kennedy

In his 1974 book, *Beyond Contract: Work, Power and Trust Relations*, Alan Fox set out the contrasting characteristics of high and low-trust relationships.

High-trust relationships

- share (or have similar) ends and values
- have a diffuse sense of long-term obligation
- offer support without calculating the cost or expecting an immediate return
- communicate freely and openly with one another
- are prepared to trust the other and risk their own fortunes in the other party
- give the benefit of the doubt in relation to motives and goodwill if there are problems

Low-trust relationships

- have divergent goals
- have explicit expectations, which must be reciprocated through balanced exchanges
- carefully calculate the cost and benefits of any concession made
- restrict and screen communications in their own separate interests

- attempt to minimise their dependence on the other's discretion
- are suspicious about mistakes or failure, attributing them to ill will or default and invoke sanctions

One of the most useful bits of reading on leadership and management is the last twelve pages of *In Search of Excellence* by Peters and Waterman, in which they set out the properties of Loose-Tight leadership: "It is in essence the coexistence of firm central direction and maximum individual autonomy." The idea is that organisations work best when there is a combination of firm central direction expressed through value systems and "rigidly shared values." For example, attention to the customer, quality, focus on the people, and maximum autonomy at operational level. So, provided you do things in the way they are done round here, you have the freedom to make things happen in the way that works best in your situation. Operational managers flourish under these circumstances. They know what they have to do and they know that they can do the rest in the way it needs to be done.

A good example of Loose-Tight leadership is the revival of Waterstone's the booksellers. James Daunt, appointed in 2011 to rescue the chain, attributes his success, in part, to giving back his managers responsibility for their own stock, allowing them "to tailor much of their stock to their customers taste." This is the "loose" within the Waterstone's "tight".

Max de Pree was an American industrialist who was much influenced by Robert Greenleaf. His book *Leadership Is an Art* includes powerful words about leadership including on the importance of "polishing, liberating and enabling the gifts of others" and about leaders bearing burdens on behalf of those they seek to lead: "Leaders don't inflict pain; they bear pain."

"Leaders do the right thing, managers do things right."
— On Becoming a Leader, *Warren Bennis, 1989*

"Real leaders move the human heart."
— *Warren Bennis and James O'Toole*

In *Managing Towards the Millennium*, edited by James E. Hennessey and Suki Robins, authoritarian and servant leaders are compared:

> Authoritarian leaders give orders and protect the concentration of power at the top of the chain of command. To them people are simply a means for achieving a purpose. In contrast the servant leader sees people as an end in themselves worthy of full development.
>
> The goal of the authoritarian leaders is to have relatively passive followers. The goal of the servant leader is to interact with active followers in such a way as to maximise their self-sufficiency and creativity to satisfy all stakeholders. The servant leader helps followers to grow, and benefits from their initiative.
>
> [...] The underlying principle of both quality and servant leadership is integrity.
>
> [...] The leader serves the worker who in turn serves the customer.

Ian Dillow, who led the excellent public relations team at the Wessex Regional Health Authority during my time as chief executive, kindly read the draft of this book and reminded me of something I had shared with him in our Wessex days:

> In the end there are probably only two types of leadership and both can be effective. The first is management by fear, when your staff will do what you want for fear of the consequences of not doing so. The second is management with care, and even affection, for your staff. The difference between these two types is that when things go wrong, as they almost always will, the manager who manages by fear looks over his shoulder to find there is no one there. The manager who manages with affection finds all his staff lined up behind him.

Peter Griffiths is one of the most able and experienced health services managers and his advice is born out of experience at the very highest levels as deputy chief executive of the NHS, a regional general manager, first chief executive of the Guys and Lewisham NHS trust, chief executive of the Health Quality Service, chairman of the Queen Victoria NHS Trust and chairman of the Foundation Trust Network. Here are some wise words from Peter, taken from his presidential address to the Institute of Health Services in 1995:

The characteristics of managers and professionals across the NHS who do display the leadership dimension in their management work can be summarised as follows:

- They have a passion for the service they are providing and ensure the maintenance of high standards.
- They are constantly dissatisfied and looking for improvement.
- They are as interested in the outcomes of what their service achieves as much as the inputs to it.
- They have an openness to learn from different perspectives and positively value diversity and difference.
- They seek consensus as well as having strong ideas of their own and value dialogue as well as debate.
- They are able to admit their mistakes and encourage others to do likewise as they see this as an essential feature of learning and improving.
- They are profoundly concerned with the treatment of people and regard the selection, motivation, retention and occasional termination of people from their organisations as the most important thing to try to get right.
- They regard their people as the most critical source of ideas and information about how to do a better job and the most important source of information about what users feel about the service they are receiving.
- They are concerned with visioning, but not in the sense of visions being hallucinations, rather through involving people in painting a picture of a new tomorrow based on the realities and concerns of today.
- They regard the relationship with their professional colleagues, notably doctors and nurses, as being crucial to the delivery of effective health services and they view the perspective that clinicians bring to bear about individuals as vital to the process of corporate decision-making.

John P. Kotter is one of the people whose thinking has influenced me most. His book *What Leaders Really Do* is very valuable. Kotter deals with the difference between leadership and management, the importance of behaviour based on a "moral framework" Kotter's description of change is the most helpful I have ever come across.

The 8-Step Process of Change[81]

- Create a sense of urgency.
- Put together a strong team to direct process.
- Create an appropriate vision.
- Communicate that vision broadly.
- Empower employees to act on that vision.
- Deliver sufficient short-term results to give credibility and disempower cynics.
- Build momentum and use it to tackle tough change.
- Anchor behaviour in organisational culture.

"Level 5 leaders blend the paradoxical combination of deep personal humility with intense professional will."

"How do Level 5 leaders manifest humility? They routinely credit others, external factors and good luck for their company's success. But when results are poor, they blame themselves. They also act quietly, calmly, and determinedly – relying on inspired standards, not inspiring charisma, to motivate."
— Level 5 Leadership: The Triumph of Humility and Fierce Resolve,
Jim Collins in Harvard Business Review

"Many men have discovered that, however satisfying it is in the short run, the urge to be better than, to dominate and control, brings only emptiness and despair."

81:    Kotter, John. Leading Change: Why Transformation Efforts Fail. *Harvard Business Review* (March–April 1995)

"Ultimately, for both men and women, heroism is a matter of integrity, of becoming more and more themselves at each stage of their development."
— The Hero Within, *Carol S. Pearson (1986)*

"A true master is not one with the most students, but one who creates the most masters. A true leader is not the one with the most followers, but one who creates the most leaders. A true king is not the one with the most subjects, but the one who leads the most to royalty. A true teacher is not the one with the most knowledge, but one who causes the most others to have knowledge."
— Conversations with God, Book 1, *Neale Donald Walsch, 1995*

Beverly Alimo-Metcalfe has had a major impact on my thinking. Beverly reminds us that "leadership is a contact sport" and that we need to ask ourselves if those we serve grow as people. She suggests that leaders and managers should be "obsessed with values" and live them "inside out" and should connect what they do with who they are and those they serve. She also says, "A leader is someone who has more belief in others than they have in themselves – the keeper of the faith until they come to believe it for themselves."

Beverley's research has very helpful things to say about leadership and culture in high performing teams. The conclusions are particularly helpful when looked at alongside Michael West's work on effective teamwork, discussed in Chapter Two.

Characteristics of leadership in high performing teams[82]

- engaging important stakeholders
- collective vision of good-quality service
- non-hierarchical teams
- supportive culture
- successful change management

82:   Alimo-Metcalfe, B. et. al. 'The Impact of Engaging Leadership on Performance, Attitudes to Work and Well-being at Work: A Longitudinal Study'. *Journal of Health and Organizational Management*, vol 22, pp 586–98 (2008)

The culture of highly productive teams is characterised by:

- staff feel involved in developing the vision
- staff feel involved in determining how to achieve the vision
- staff feel empowered by being trusted to take decisions
- staff feel actively supported in developing their strengths
- staff believe their ideas will be listened to
- time is made for staff to discuss problems and issues, despite the busy schedule
- there is high use of face-to-face communication

Beverly Alimo-Metcalfe and John Alban-Metcalfe conducted the largest ever investigation into leadership (management) in the NHS and found that the staff gave the highest ratings to the managers for focusing effort and being decisive. The lowest scores were for:
- inspiring others
- supporting a developmental culture
- showing genuine concern
- being honest and consistent
- acting with integrity

Showing genuine concern was found to be the single most important indicator of transformational leadership.[83]

Caring to Change: How Compassionate Leadership Can Stimulate Innovation in Health Care is a powerful contribution to the thinking on leadership. Many of the themes are similar to the values and behaviours discussed in this book. I wish that I had been able to read this work at a much earlier stage in my journey of experience and learning.[84]

83: Alimo-Metcalfe, B and Alban-Metcalfe, J. Stamp of Greatness. *Health Services Journal* (June 2003)

84: West, M. et al. Caring to Change: How Compassionate Leadership Can Stimulate Innovation in Health Care. King's Fund (2017)

20182793R00059

Printed in Great Britain
by Amazon